PETRARCH'S
BOOK WITHOUT A NAME

A Translation of the
LIBER SINE NOMINE

by

Norman P. ZACOUR
University of Toronto

THE PONTIFICAL INSTITUTE OF MEDIAEVAL STUDIES
TORONTO CANADA
1973

to Charles J. Mackenzie

TABLE OF CONTENTS

FOREWORD

The papal court of Avignon came in for a good deal of criticism in its day, and has not had too good a press since. There were English complaints about its favouritism toward the French, Italian complaints about its prolonged stay in Avignon, episcopal complaints about its continual interference in local church affairs, and individual complaints about the avarice of its officials, all of which and more find an echo in modern historical literature. Nothing, however, compares in the scope of its polemic with Petrarch's *Liber sine nomine*. More important, whether he is directly cited or not his opinions have nearly always coloured modern interpretations of the Avignonese papacy. It is difficult, however, to weigh these opinions out of context, and it has therefore seemed to me a useful task to provide a complete translation of the *Liber sine nomine* so that one might the more easily test the temper of the work as a whole before coming to any conclusions about how balanced Petrarch's assessment may have been.

I should like to thank Rev. L.E. Boyle, O.P., of the Pontifical Institute of Mediaeval Studies, and the readers of the Institute's press for many valuable comments and corrections. The shortcomings that remain, however, are either Petrarch's or mine.

Toronto
May 7, 1971.

N.P.Z.

INTRODUCTION

"To forgive those who injure you is a splendid kind of revenge; to ignore them altogether, more splendid still."[1] Petrarch was in his last year of life, an old man of seventy, when he proferred this bit of wisdom to the young lord of Padua, Francesco da Carrara. Forgive and forget—it was not the sort of counsel that he himself would have listened to some fifteen years earlier when he was putting the finishing touches to his *Liber sine nomine*, the secret collection of nineteen letters presented below in translation. The work was to be his indictment of the papal court and the society of Avignon, the new Babylon, whose offences he would never forgive and had no intention of letting us forget. On more than one occasion he even spoke of writing a full-scale poetic tragedy on the theme of courtly corruption in the papal city, setting down word for word what Truth herself might dictate, and leaving the sordid tale to be judged by us: "You, Posterity, you be the judge, unless, as it happens, you are so overwhelmed by the evils of your own day that you cannot be bothered with ours."[2]

He had his hands full with other literary undertakings when he wrote this, however, and the idea of a *carmen tragicum* was to remain stillborn. "If I were to start on this Babylonian history in which I am incessantly involved," he grumbled to Boccaccio, "it will be a vain undertaking, since I've put so much of it already into my letters to friends."[3] And so instead of composing a finished

---

[1] *Epistolae seniles*, XIV, 1, in *Francisci Petrarchae Florentini... opera quae extant omnia* (Basle, 1554), I, 422 (the letter is printed separately from the *epistolae seniles* under the title *De republica optime administranda liber*).
[2] See below, letter 6.
[3] *Fam.* XII, 10, Rossi III, 33-34.

work on the subject he preserved the letters themselves, which he called *Liber sine nomine* — *liber*, not *epistolae*, for he thought of the letters as a unit, not merely a collection of items. To be sure, Posterity was far too overwhelmed by its own troubles to pay much attention to it, but it found a place, of course, in the several editions of his collected works which appeared in the fifteenth and sixteenth centuries, and letter 18, which ranged from a denunciation of the apocalyptic whore of Babylon to a racy tale of old cardinal and young courtesan was too good a piece of anti-clerical propaganda to escape sixteenth-century translation into German and Italian. On the whole, however, the work fell into obscurity, and it even became possible to maintain that Petrarch was not its author — that he could not have been guilty of such scandalous stuff — and that the entire collection was the work of a heretic impostor.[4] It was not until the nineteenth-century revival of interest in Petrarch as an Italian nationalist that the work began to receive sustained attention. Giuseppe Fracassetti, who did more than any other scholar to rescue Petrarch's correspondence from obscurity, heroically reconstituting the various collections of his letters to make them available not only in their original Latin but, for a wider public, in Italian translation, still boggled at the *Sine nomine*. "It seems to me," he wrote, "that those who do not hesitate to offer to the public what he [Petrarch] had kept secret and denied to casual view do a disservice to the reputation of their author ...... I have rejected all thought of bringing out an edition or restoring the text of these letters, as being unworthy of a Catholic and a Franciscan tertiary."[5] There were others, however, who were readier to make the collection available. It was translated in its entirety into French in 1885 and into Italian ten years later,[6] at which

---

[4] Abraham BZOVIUS, *Ann. Eccl.*, ad an. 1347, col. 1014; cf. col. 1013, and also ad an. 1355, col. 1204.

[5] *Francisci Petrarcae epistolae de rebus familiaribus et variae*, I (Florence: Le Monnier, 1859), v. He expresses similar sentiments in his introduction to his translations, *Lettere di Francesco Petrarca*, I (Florence: Le Monnier, 1863), 29.

[6] Victor DEVELAY, *Pétrarque: Lettres sans titre* (Paris, 1885).
Orazio d'UVA, *Le Anepigrafe di Fr. Petrarca* (Sassari, 1895).

time also the collection received its first thorough-going study of any real value.[7]

These and other occasional translations of individual letters had to be made, however, from single and usually defective texts. It was only in 1925 that Paul Piur provided a text based on an exhaustive examination of all available manuscripts, accompanying it with a study not only of the contents of the letters (having to do with the question of addressees, dates, and the like), but also a lengthy discussion of the historical and intellectual milieu within which Petrarch lived and worked, and something, too, of his psychological make-up. It is Piur's text that has been used for this translation.[8]

PETRARCH[9]

Francesco Petrarca was born on July 20, 1304, in Arezzo, the son of a Florentine notary who had been exiled from Florence as a result of the political upheavals of that city only two years earlier. By 1312 Petrarch's father had abandoned hope of returning to Florence and regaining his confiscated property, and the family moved to Provence where the recent establishment of the papacy in Avignon promised employment. Petrarch was about eight years old when he first saw the city that he was to make infamous as the new Babylon. He grew up in Carpentras, a town about 15 miles from Avignon, in the company of other Italian expatriates, where

[7] G. BRIZZOLARA, "Le Sine Titulo di Petrarca," *Studi storici*, IV (1895), 1-42, 447-471.

[8] Paul PIUR, *Petrarcas 'Buch ohne Namen' und die päpstliche Kurie: Ein Beitrag zur Geistesgeschichte der Frührenaissance* (Halle/Saale: Max Niemeyer, 1925).

[9] There are many biographies of Petrarch. The most recent is also the best, Morris BISHOP, *Petrarch and His World* (Bloomington: Indiana University Press, 1963). Ernest Hatch WILKINS, *Life of Petrarch* (Chicago: University of Chicago Press, 1961) is less satisfactory to read because of its strict chronological arrangement which makes it impossible for the author to discuss any particular matter at length. Nevertheless it is impeccably accurate, an indispensable tool for anyone interested in Petrarch's life and work.

he also received his first schooling. At the age of twelve he was sent by his father to acquire a legal education, first to Montpellier and then later to the great law university of Bologna. His student days came to an end some ten years later when his father died; now he closed his law books and abandoned all thought of pursuing what he had come to consider a tedious and distasteful career.

Indeed, during much of the time that he was studying the Digest of Justinian and its many glosses, with considerable promise as he himself tells us, he was also developing a strong interest in classical literature — he was a precocious Latinist — and in writing Italian poetry, quite the fashion in Bologna at the time. On his return to Avignon after his father's death he led for some time a life of dissolution, to judge from his later rueful remarks on his wasted youth, writing love poems, dressing according to fashion, curling his hair, chasing women, and running through his inheritance. Now, too, he first met Laura whose identity he would carefully disguise but whose name he was to immortalize in his sonnets and who was to remain for him a poetic inspiration of great power. Their relationship was a platonic one, more Laura's doing than Petrarch's, for which he would later be grateful. Even after her death during the plague of 1348 she continued to live on in bitter-sweet memory, and for the next ten years on each anniversary of her death (April 6) he would write a special commemorative poem.

Petrarch soon ran short of money — there are vague hints that he and his younger brother Gherardo were somehow cheated out of their inheritance — and he had to look about for some source of income. He might have taken up the law again, but instead preferred to enter on an ecclesiastical career, to take lower orders, seek the patronage of an ecclesiastic, and solicit appointment to some church benefice or other, some canonry perhaps, the income from which might allow him a sufficient living. He was fortunate in his friendship with Giacomo Colonna, whom he had met at the university of Bologna. Giacomo was a member of the powerful Colonna family of Rome, and through his connections in the papal court, where his brother Giovanni was a cardinal, he had been given the bishopric of Lombez. It was through Giacomo that Petrarch came to the attention of Cardinal Giovanni whose service he entered in 1330 as a chaplain, presumably performing secretarial duties, and it was the cardinal who recommended him for a papal appointment to a canonry in Giacomo's church of Lombez in 1335. In subsequent years Petrarch acquired additional such appointments which eased the financial strain and eventually left him independent.[10] He could devote himself more and more to those pursuits which were to become for him a full-time career, especially the study of the Latin classics, the composition of Latin works of prose and poetry (he gradually abandoned writing in the vernacular), and the collection of the finest library of classical works to be found in the fourteenth century.

Even though he was nominally one of the cardinal's chaplains, Petrarch was left almost entirely free not only to immerse himself in his studies but also to indulge a restless nature in travel. He had passed through the Midi to spend a memorable summer with Giacomo Colonna and other friends in Lombez beneath the Pyrenees in 1330. Three years later the Cardinal allowed him to go north where he visited Paris, the Lowlands and the Rhine valley. It was during this journey, while in Liège, that he turned up two orations of Cicero. At the end of 1336 he was off again, this time to Rome as a guest of the Colonna family, a welcome escape from Avignon on hearing the news that he would soon be presented with an illegitimate child (it was a boy). He had already developed a strong aversion for Avignon — how strong it would eventually become will be apparent on reading the letters below. On his return from Rome in 1337 he was fortunate, therefore, in being able to buy, probably with the help and certainly with the permission of Cardinal Giovanni, a small country-

[10] E.H. WILKINS, "Petrarch's Ecclesiastical Career," *Speculum*, XXVIII (1953), 754-775; reprinted in E.H. WILKINS, *Studies in the Life and Works of Petrarch* (Cambridge: Mediaeval Academy of America, 1955), pp. 3-32.

house in Vaucluse, about 15 miles from Avignon, which allowed him
to escape the shameless city, avoid confronting the woman he had
wronged, and seek in solitude, though with little success, some
alleviation of the obsessive pain caused by continually seeing
his unattainable Laura.

Petrarch was happy in his new-found haven from the demands
of Avignon. "Where, outside of Italy, can I find greater
tranquility?" he asks.[11] He spent many quiet, carefree days in
Vaucluse, wandering in the fields, listening to the songs of birds,
the sounds of the river and the voices of the muses, rejoicing
in the companionship of his many books, happy for the moment to
be free from the tedium of urban *voluptates* and the eternal bowing
and scraping of the court. Vaucluse would inspire one of his most
readable works, the *De vita solitaria*, begun in 1346 though not
finished until twenty years later. In it he draws a strong contrast
between the fruitful quiet of rural solitude and the frightful din
of city life, in all of which it is not difficult to see Vaucluse and
Avignon.

In Petrarch, however, there was a constant tension between a
fastidiousness which shrank from the crowded and noisy life of
the city, and a consuming ambition for fame which drove him back
again and again into the world of great men and great affairs, that
world which he despised all the more for his own dependence on
it. He solicited and received invitations from both the
university of Paris and the city of Rome (he would accept the
latter's) to be crowned with the laurel wreath in imitation of the
ancient form of recognizing poetic merit, and in 1341 he went
to Naples to sit a three-day examination at the hands of King
Robert — who but a king could examine Petrarch? — before
going on to the coronation ceremony on the Capitoline in Rome
where he would hear a Roman senator deliver in his honour
a laudatory address which he himself had helped to prepare. He was

[11] *Fam*. VI, 3, Rossi II, 76.

back again in Naples two years later, commissioned by the pope to seek the release from prison of some rebels against the crown. He prolonged these periods of absence from Avignon as much as possible, lingered in Rome over the many sites reminiscent of the ancient glory of the city, warmed himself before the glowing praise of newly-met friends in Naples, and then spent long months in Parma lionized by the ruling Correggi. In fact he even bought a house in Parma with the idea of abandoning Avignon altogether, but the fall from power of the Correggi upset his plans and he had to return to Provence.

While there he stayed as close to Vaucluse as possible. He begins one of his sonnets thus: "From impious Babylon whence every sense of shame has fled, every good departed, from the abode of grief and mother of errors, I have fled for my life. Here I am alone..." (no. 114). He rarely went in to Avignon except on the most pressing business, such as the legitimization of his son by the pope. A man of great distinction in the world of letters, he could no longer feel comfortable at the beck and call of a master, even if that master was his great benefactor Cardinal Giovanni Colonna. Their relations grew cool, Petrarch's service to the cardinal virtually came to an end, and when he again went to Italy in November, 1347 (as he thought, never to return), there was a final rancorous break. The next year the cardinal died.

Petrarch returned to Italy to be installed in a canonry in the church of Parma which the cardinal had generously helped him to get from the pope, and in which he now intended to take up permanent residence. The Parmese appointment gave him the opportunity to escape a city which he had come to hate, and to return to an Italy which he had always loved, now astir with news of the great revolution in Rome led by Cola di Rienzo. Parma was not, however, as peaceful a place as he had hoped it would be. He soon fell out with his bishop, for what reason we do not know. So for the next four years he passed up no chance of travelling, to Padua as guest of its ruler Jacopo da Ferrara where he would obtain another canonry, to Rome as a pilgrim during the jubilee of 1350, to Mantua, Vergil's birthplace, where he first discovered Pliny's *Natural History*, to Florence, Arezzo, Ferrara, Verona — surprisingly, in the summer of 1351, to Avignon again. Why did he go back? Once at the papal court he was able to perform various services for his friends, but none of these were so important as to demand a special trip to that city which he hated so much. His own story is that he returned to Avignon because he had been summoned by two cardinals to see the pope, about what they did not tell him. Given his feelings about the papal court, however, it is hard to believe that he would freely go there without any idea of why he was doing so. That he expected to take on some weighty responsibility seems evident from letter 8 below, written to his friend the bishop of Padua who had urged him to stay away from Avignon and not to be governed by ambition. It has been conjectured, with good reason, that Petrarch thought that he was going to receive a cardinal's hat.[12] Instead, much to his disgust, he was asked to take on the job of papal secretary with the rank of bishop, an offer he had refused before and now refused again. If he had any suspicion, he says, that this was why he had been asked to come back (surely revealing that he expected something much greater), he would never have bothered.

The return to Provence was not all loss. He had left a large library and some important unfinished works in Vaucluse, and concern for these undoubtedly played some part in his decision to go back. Between his literary work in Vaucluse and his excursions into Avignon to further some petition or other (he was successful in getting from Pope Clement a church benefice for his son Giovanni), he was kept busy. He also continued to follow affairs in Rome with great interest, and showed much concern for the fate of Cola di Rienzo (see below, letter 4). He willingly responded to an invitation to set down his views for a commission of four cardinals which the pope had set up to review the

---

[12] E.H. WILKINS, *Studies in the Life and Works of Petrarch*, pp. 63-80.

problem of the government of Rome. He also urged the emperor, Charles IV, to enter Italy and reestablish peace and harmony in the troubled peninsula. Even so, it is difficult to account for references to his being used up, worn out, exhausted, as he describes himself in letter 5, to his many duties and his preoccupation with his disordered affairs (6), or to his many demanding duties and cares (11), except as expressions of an author impatient to get back to his desk and therefore doubly exasperated by the niggling affairs of court.

Petrarch had sufficient experience of Avignon over the years to account for any amount of reasoned criticism he might make of the papal court and city. But it was this final stay, from the summer of 1351 to May 1353, which brought his growing revulsion to a head, accounting for the kind of attack on the papacy, the college of cardinals, and the French predominance in the papal court which is the particular mark of the *Sine nomine*. It is now that we get the fevered hyperbole that sets this collection apart.

THE SINE NOMINE

By 1350, influenced by Cicero's letter-collection which he himself had discovered in Verona just five years earlier, Petrarch had conceived of the idea of publishing a grand collection of his own letters. He began by writing a dedicatory letter to his friend "Socrates," the Fleming Ludwig van Kempen who, like Petrarch himself, had been in the household of Cardinal Giovanni Colonna. The letter to Socrates was to serve as a preface to what he tentatively called *Epistolarum mearum ad diversos liber* but which was finally entitled *Epistolae familiares*. He continued during the next several years to carry on an increasingly large correspondence, now consciously writing his letters with an eye to future publication and keeping copies of them much more carefully than he had done hitherto (he mentions to Socrates the thousand or more letters and poems he had earlier burned). As the collection grew in bulk he re-ordered it, made stylistic and other changes, broke large letters

up into smaller ones, included fictional letters written only for
the collection, fiddled and fussed over a thousand little changes
in preparation for ultimate publication. A good deal of this editorial
work was done during his last stay in Provence, 1351-1353, the
period in which he also wrote most of those letters which would
eventually form the *Liber sine nomine.*
By 1358-1359, now in Milan, he considered the collection
finished, and in the spring of 1359 he had a certain *ingeniosus
homo et amicus* transcribe the whole collection onto parchment, thus
forming an archetype which by the following year, what with late
additions and the inclusion of a special group of fictional letters
he had earlier written to ancient authors (Cicero, Vergil and others),
came to twenty books. Another copy was made around 1363-1364;
then in 1366 he added some letters he had written in the interval,
bringing the work to its final form in twenty-four books containing
350 letters.
A lot of sorting went into the preparation of the archetype.
There were many letters which Petrarch either had lost his copy
of, or had destroyed, or for one reason or another deliberately
decided to exclude from the *Familiares*, some 59 of which were
collected by Giuseppe Fracassetti and published under the title
Litterae variae.[13] But there were some others still that Petrarch was
too fond of to abandon, yet whose inclusion in the *Familiares*
spelled trouble, so he decided to make a small separate collection
of them. By pulling them together instead of leaving them scattered
throughout the *Familiares*, Petrarch says, he could make it easy
for any reader whom they angered to destroy them without
disrupting the larger collection — a transparent conceit. The real
advantage was Petrarch's, for his *Familiares* would receive a more
generous reception without these letters than with them, and he
could avoid the criticism that they were bound to arouse by
holding up their publication until after his death.

---

[13] In the third volume of his *Francisci Petrarcae epistolae de rebus familiaribus et
variae*, 3 vols. (Florence: Le Monnier, 1859-1863).

Of course, Petrarch could not be sure of keeping them hidden. He had already had some unfortunate experiences with overzealous friends quick to circulate anything of his they could get their hands on. So in case the letters did get about he took the further precaution of removing from them all traces of the identities of those to whom they had been written. He wanted to save his correspondents from embarrassment or worse. Hence the title of the work, *Sine nomine.* In fact, Petrarch went even further. There are no names of contemporaries anywhere in the book. The only names to be found are those of classical, biblical and mythical figures, and of ancient authors.

We need not look far for the principles that determined which letters would go into the *Sine nomine,* or rather would be kept out of the *Familiares.* We can take his own explanation at face value, that he held back those letters that were likely to bring the larger collection into disrepute. He also claims that he selected those letters whose recipients, dead or alive, had to be protected from injury or calumny. Surely, however, this could not be the reason for holding up publication, say, of the letters to Cola di Rienzo (2 and 3) or the letter to the Roman people (4). Petrarch kept these out of the *Familiares* only to save himself from embarrassment, since they not only revealed the extent to which he supported Cola but were extremely critical of papal policy respecting the city of Rome, and of powerful forces in the papal court.

The large collection of *Familiares,* therefore, is generally restrained respecting the papacy and the mode of life in Avignon. It is not, however, completely devoid of critical comments. It includes, for example, a long letter to an Italian cardinal in which Petrarch spoke out vigorously against the wealth of members of the sacred college. Here are a few selections.

I know you're surprised that I should wish today to inflict, so uncustomarily, this — shall we call it inconvenient? — philosophy on you. But I address myself no more to you than to almost all men, and those of your order *(tuum genus)* amongst whom especially, it seems to me, imperious Greed has succeeded in raising her throne and has firmly planted her banner. I am all the more indignant since there is all the less reason for your cupidity. For whom do you heap up these piles of gold, you who cannot have legitimate heirs? You stand revealed before the eyes of the world, pointed to by all people in sharp disapproval. "Look at those preachers of virtue," they say, "They give pretty sermons about the life eternal and the soul freed by death, but they themselves are slaves of avarice, unaccountably devoted to the things of this world."

For whom do you heap up riches, unless for the devil and his minions, who watch over you with care, number your days, and most anxiously await your inheritance? Out of the money you have wrested from the poor they will erect most grateful monuments on the portal of Tartarus inscribed with your names.[14]

This is not the only letter in the *Familiares* to adopt such a disapproving tone, but it is on the whole rather exceptional. Throughout the collection there are references to the unbearable life in Avignon, but they are brief enough, and scattered enough, to pass for a kind of conventional complaint not dissimilar to the *Invective in curiales* which would become a familiar *topos* of humanist literature in the late fourteenth and fifteenth centuries. "There is nothing uglier, nothing more incredible," he says of Avignon in 1339. The pope "has deserted his proper see (against nature, I do believe), and strives to act the head of the world, forgetful of the Lateran and Sylvester"[15] (1342). "I couldn't stand that sewer of a court" (1348). "I shall begin to live and prosper again when I find the exit from this labyrinth" (1352). "You know how much the Babylonian court delighted me when the place was less foul and we were younger," he reminds a friend; now those who were once avid to go there are all the more avid to escape (1352). When he was about to leave Avignon for the last time, in 1353, he says that just so long as he is not in Babylon he will accept whatever Fate decrees. A few years later there will be a reference to the

---

[14] *Fam*. VI, 1, Rossi II, 47-54, esp. p. 50ff.

[15] Forgetting, that is, that the Lateran was bestowed on pope Sylvester I by a secular ruler, the emperor Constantine the Great.

reputation of what others call *parva Roma* but what he calls *novissima Babylon*, as being so widespread as to be well known even to the Arabs and the Indians.[16] Strung together in this way these comments take on greater force than they actually possess in context. It is all rather tame stuff compared with what went into the *Sine nomine*, as we shall see.

We need not rely on this general restraint of the *Familiares* to indicate that Petrarch was careful to protect himself. In a letter to the archbishop of Prague in 1357 he frankly conceded that while "fear never forces a brave man to lie, it sometimes compels him to keep quiet,"[17] precisely the sentiment which seems to have decided which letters were to be kept out of the *Familiares*.

ROME AND AVIGNON

Petrarch's principle of selection has given the *Liber sine nomine* a marked thematic unity. In effect the work treats of two cities, Rome and Avignon, two women, so to speak, the one majestic, dignified, slowly rousing herself from long slumber, soberly reaching out to reclaim her sceptre, the other a cheeky harlot queening it over the world, heedless of her impending doom.

The scene for this tale of two cities was first set by the Gascon pope Clement V (1305-1314), pitifully subservient to the French crown, who never got to Rome as he had hoped and promised, and whose foot-loose and fragmented court finally found temporary shelter in Carpentras and Avignon. His successor John XXII (1316-1334) centralized the scattered court in Avignon where he himself used to be bishop. There he took up residence in his old episcopal palace, a temporary expedient before moving to Bologna and then to Rome. He had no more success, however, than his

[16] The citations are from *Fam.* III, 11, Rossi I, 127; *Fam.* VI, 6, Rossi II, 72; *Fam.* VII, 11, Rossi II, 116; *Fam.* XII, 10, Rossi III, 34; *Fam.* XV, 8, Rossi III, 155; Fam. XVI, 10, Rossi III, 202; *Fam.* XV, 7, Rossi III, 150.

[17] *Fam.* XXI, 1, Rossi IV, 51.

predecessor in pacifying war-torn Italy, an essential first step
to a return to Rome. Benedict XII (1334-1342) decided that papal
residence in Avignon was going to be long indeed, and con-
structed a fortress-like palace to provide more permanent and
more convenient accommodation for those conducting the heavy
business of the court; and Clement VI (1342-1352) not only built a
large addition to the palace but in 1348 purchased title to the city
of Avignon from its secular ruler Queen Joan of Naples.
Talk of a move to Rome became increasingly unreal, dream-like.

What gave to the establishment of the papacy in Avignon an even
greater appearance of permanency was the change in the complexion
of the papal court itself. A succession of popes from southern France
soon brought in train a curial personnel predominantly French
— auditors, scriptors and other officials and employees both secular
and ecclesiastic — for whom a move to Rome would represent
exile to a foreign, hostile, unhealthy and dangerous land. The
Italian component of the court shrank rapidly, not alone in the
pope's personal service, for as Italian cardinals died they were
replaced by French cardinals each of whom brought to the court,
or soon drew there, a large household of advisers and servants
nearly all of whom were also French — relatives, friends, friends
of relatives, relatives of friends — who now commanded the
lion's share of the immense patronage in ecclesiastical benefices at
the disposition of the court. Only as notaries could the Italians
manage to hold their own, testimony to the outstanding reputation
of Italian notarial training and experience, but even here, in the
later years of the Avignonese papacy, the French began to make
inroads.

There remained, therefore, an Italian colony in Avignon, gradually diminishing through attrition, too small to exert any real
influence as a group, clinging for protection and preferment to
the robes of the two or three Italians in the college of cardinals.
Yet it was large enough, we may imagine, to retain a strong sense
of identity and allow unhappy exiles to reinforce one another's
resentment over their unequal treatment, share experiences of real

or imagined slights at the hands of the French, and dream of
that happier day to come when the natural order of things might
be restored. The reader will find much of this reflected in the
Sine nomine.

We should do Petrarch a large injustice, however, if we were
to think of him merely as the voice of disgruntled expatriates. He
was undoubtedly on firm ground in damning the immorality of
Avignon. But he was moved by more than moral outrage alone.
His attitude was reinforced by a political theory derived in large
part from a romantic reading of Roman history, viewing Rome as
the centre of the ecclesiastical and secular universe, and looking
to the unification of Italy as the necessary corollary of Rome's
rule. All this was to be brought into being by a common act
of will. The intervening centuries fall away, and the Romans
to whom Petrarch writes (see letter 4) are again those whose
great deeds Livy once recorded. Petrarch's views of Avignon and
Rome could proceed together, therefore, without conflict — the
one growing from his stance as a moral philosopher, the other
from his proto-nationalism. He was fortunate that the papal court
was not in fact re-established in Rome during his lifetime and was not
dominated again by Italians. What a quandary he would have been
in!

Avignon and Rome were more than just cities. They were cosmic
emanations, the one a disruption of nature, a kind of aberrant
chaos, the other a divine order rooted in history. This is the
theme of the *Liber sine nomine.* The work cannot, therefore, be
treated as a sober piece of social description, to be used literally
for a reconstruction of life at the time. The letters had no circulation,
could neither be confirmed nor contradicted nor corrected by contemporaries, and were consigned to Posterity as such a vague bill of
particulars that their use as historical documents becomes extremely
hazardous. For those who wish to make a case against the pre-
Reformation papacy, against the "Babylonian Captivity," what a
storehouse of devastating comment; for those who wish to rescue
the popes of Avignon from general obloquy, what belchings of a

disordered digestion; but for those who wish to do neither, what a revelation of Petrarch himself!

How bitter his experience, how great his humiliation, how deep his hatred, to arouse such invective as this! Yet we have only hints, no details, of the many incidents which must have caused him such pain, having to solicit favours from greedy bureaucrats, to conceal his feelings of disgust with the manners of those on whom he was dependent, unceasingly revolted by a society which constantly reminded him of his own youthful follies, his own sensuality, his own ambition; having to disguise his contempt for those in power whom he felt were inferior beings, insane barbarians lording it over civilized people. How he ached for revenge. And the crowning indignity was that such animals actually sneer at their rightful masters! He cannot believe it. Their contempt must be a cover for their fear. Anything else is unthinkable.

It was impossible, therefore, and for that matter beside the point, for Petrarch to make a cool assessment of the merits and shortcomings of the papal court, such as that of Nicolas de Clamanges, for example, who wrote at the end of the century:

Though I have no wish to absolve that [papal] court of its vices, still there was a greater modesty of manners to be found there, a greater kind of honesty, a greater seriousness in the performance of their duties, than can be found in the courts of secular princes, where everything today is in terrible disarray.[18]

It was not Petrarch's purpose to indulge the timidity of historians with such cautious compromise, but rather to champion Truth.

---

[18] Ezio ORNATO, *Jean Muret et ses amis Nicolas de Clamanges et Jean de Montreuil* (Geneva/ Paris: Droz, 1969), p. 58.

LIBER SINE NOMINE

PREFACE

Though truth has always been hated, it is now a capital
crime. No doubt the hatred of truth has grown and flattery
and falsehood now reign supreme because of the growing
sins of mankind. I recall often having said this, and sometimes even writing it, but it ought to be said and written
more often. The lament will not cease before the pain
departs. This idea led me some time ago to write the
Bucolicum carmen, a kind of cryptic poem which, though
understood only by a few, might possibly please many; for
some people have a taste for letters so corrupt that the well-
known, no matter how sweet its flavour, offends them,
while every mystery, no matter how sour, charms them.
Strange, how it's the weak who so often look for troubles
to shoulder.

The same reflection on truth led me today to finish up,
with this preface, a few items of mine — few indeed, though
the truer they are the more hateful they will be to evil men,
but attractive to good men, if I am not mistaken. I refer to
some letters written to friends on different matters and at
various times. I have assembled them in a single collection
so that they would not, being scattered as they were, sully
the whole body of my correspondence and make it hateful
to the enemies of truth; and so that whoever wants to read
them may know where to find them, and whoever doesn't
may know what to avoid. Then, too, if anyone decides that
they should be obliterated or suppressed, he can the more

easily destroy them as a unit without wrecking the entire collection. I quite deliberately planned it this way, not only for the reader but also for myself; thus I could remain safe by the obscurities and omissions of this work as I was in the deliberate vagueness of the little pastoral work I just mentioned — and not I alone, but also those to whom I wrote these letters. I have quite purposely concealed their names,[1] for if their identities were to come out into the open they would be injured if still alive or hated if dead, as though I had by preference written the letters to them knowing ahead of time that they would give them a very willing reception.

In fact, that book[2] once fell into the hands of some high-ranking personages while I was present; when they read the part that especially concerned them[3] I remember their asking what I had meant, and I intentionally changed the subject. But since this collection has no veil of similar kind, I shall do everything I can to keep it from falling into the hands of any such persons during my lifetime. If I fail, I shall not fear to be hated because of my fondness for truth, and I shall count an envy so earned as one of my proudest titles. If I succeed, then it will honestly remain hidden until I die.[4] After that, let them rant and rave, thunder and flash as much as they like. So what? If, as the Satirist says, it is safe for the living to talk about the dead,[5] surely it is much

---

[1] For the title of the work, *sine nomine*, see above p. 21.

[2] The *Bucolicum carmen*. It has been edited by Antonio Avena, *Il Bucolicum carmen e i suoi commenti inediti* (Padua, 1906).

[3] Probably Eclogue 7, entitled *Grex infectus et suffectus*, which denounces many of the cardinals during the pontificate of pope Clement VI. See E.H. Wilkins, *Studies in the Life and Works of Petrarch*, pp. 48-62.

[4] It did.

[5] JUVENAL, *Sat.* I, 162ff.

safer for the dead to talk about the living. In the first case, there may be someone alive to take revenge; but in the second, the one on whom revenge might be had no longer exists. Though his truth be hateful, destructive, calamitous, "his ship is in harbour," as the comic poet says,[6] and he is safe. He has come through the final terror and despises all the threats of mortals.

If, therefore, they plan anything against me when that time comes, let them bear in mind the neat reply that the orator Plancus gave Asinius Pollio: "Only ghosts wrestle with the dead."[7] But if they do take up arms against this work, or against my other books where either my anger or their unworthiness has subjected them to my pen, they'll find out that their quarrel will not be with me but with Truth — with God as the judge and the world as witness.

---

[6] TERENCE, *Andria*, III, 480. This is probably another of the many citations of Terence in the works of Petrarch which have the status of proverbs or sayings rather than direct quotations from the comedies. See Sesto PRETE, "Plauto, Terenzio e il Petrarca," *Studi petrarcheschi*, V (1952), 85-94.

[7] PLINY, *Natural History*, preface, 31.

THE LETTERS

1

Philippe de Cabassoles, bishop of Cavaillon, to whom this letter was sent, was an intimate friend of long standing. Petrarch first met him after he bought his house just outside the village of Vaucluse in 1337. Not only was Vaucluse in Philippe's diocese, but he too had a residence there, a castle on a spur of the mountain that rises above the source of the Sorgues. The two men were about the same age, shared many interests, had much respect and affection for one another, and were quite free in their exchange of confidences, as this letter will illustrate.

It is a measure of the obscurity of the *Liber sine nomine*, however, that we still cannot be sure who the person is that Petrarch writes about in this letter, and therefore of the date of the letter. Clearly, he writes of a pope who is seriously ill and whose death is expected momentarily. Clearly, too, he credits this pope with responsibility for what he considers the catastrophic state of the church. But which pope? There are only two possibilities: Benedict XII (died April 1342) and Clement VI (died December 1352).

The letter itself is a sustained metaphor of shipwreck. It is difficult to say whether the disaster is supposed to be the result of the decline of the ship's master or of his incompetence — whether the hand on the tiller was growing slack or was stubbornly perverse. In the latter case it is hard to see why his loss should have seemed much of a disaster. But Petrarch will have it both ways: the church is foundering not only because the pope is dying, but also because of his character, because he had been a bad pope, foul-tempered, good-for-nothing, pleasure-loving, too intent on the things of this world.

On the whole, opinion seems to favour Benedict as the subject of the letter, and therefore April-May 1342 as its date. But what little evidence there is can just as easily support the contention that Petrarch was writing about Clement at a time when he was so sick that he was thought to be dying.

It has recently been suggested that Petrarch wrote the letter in 1343 when Clement was seriously ill.[1] It is not likely, however, that he sought to convince Philippe, or could have been convinced himself, that Clement had brought the church to the brink of ruin in just a little over eighteen months.[2] However, Clement was also deathly ill late in 1351. Petrarch, in January 1352, mentions that the pope was then slowly making his way back from death's doorway.[3] Now in this letter he makes the passing comment that "unskilled hands work the oars," alluding to the fact that while the pope is sick the cardinals have become considerably more prominent in the conduct of affairs — he used the figure of oarsmen elsewhere to represent cardinals.[4] Does calling them unskilled or inexperienced (*inexperti*) mean that they had only recently been made cardinals? If so, Petrarch could well have had in mind the twelve new cardinals appointed by Clement late in 1350, whom Matteo Villani would scornfully describe as *giovani*,[5] and whom Petrarch himself would severly criticize in the seventh eclogue of his *Bucolicum carmen*. In 1351 one could still loosely describe the members of the college of cardinals — decimated by the Black Death[6] and enlarged by twelve new appointments in December 1350 — as *inexperti*.

Be this as it may, the letter is a good illustration of what Petrarch meant in his preface by the obscurities and omissions designed to guarantee his safety and that of his friends.

What are you doing, good sir; what are you doing, noble father; what are you doing, I ask — what do you think? What outcome of affairs do you look for, what hope in the

---

[1] John E. WRIGLEY, "A Papal Secret Known to Petrarch," *Speculum*, XXXIX (1964), 613-634.

[2] Clement was elected pope on May 7, 1342.

[3] *Fam.* XII, 5, Rossi III, 24.

[4] *Fam.* XI, 11, Rossi II, 350.

[5] M. Villani, IV, 86 (Moutier ed., II, 282-3).

[6] Eight died in 1348, one in 1349, two in 1350.

present shipwreck? Shall we reach port, or shall we be overwhelmed in the midst of storms? The old seaman's little
boat is too small for such large waves, the wind is too
strong for the canvas, and the keel is forced deep by the
burdensome cargo. Unskilled hands work the oars. But the
helmsman, as you see, scorns the rules of seamanship and hugs
the shore, usually a very risky business for sailors. Indeed,
the fool has too much confidence in calm weather, and
fixing his gaze on the wandering stars[7] he pays no attention
to unwavering Arctos,[8] the faithful guide of ships at sea.
Meanwhile, soaked in wine, weighed down with age, and sprin-
kled with sleep-bringing dew,[9] now he nods. now dozes, now
— would that he were the only one! — falls headlong in his
sleep.[10] We have just now looked upon the pallor of him
who falls, we have now heard the cries of the wretched who
are shipwrecked, the weakened belly of the ship has burst open,
the scattered tackle now floats about on the water.[11] Oh, if only
the Father in heaven, "seeing the ship gone astray for loss of
its master, himself might steer his own vessel through the dark

---

[7] The planets. Petrarch's scorn for astrologers is well known. One manuscript of
the *sine nomine* has the word "cardinales" written as an interlinear gloss above
the word "stellas" (PIUR, *Petrarcas "Buch ohne Namen"*, p. 286).

[8] The north star.

[9] *Soporifero rore perfusus.* The sick pope may have been under sedation. The
soporific sponge was well known to the medieval medical practitioner; for a
recipe, see the surgical treatise of Theodoric Borgognoni, O.P. (1205-1298),
which he composed while he was pope Innocent IV's penitentiary and later
revised when he was bishop of Bitonto (1262-1266): *The Surgery of Theodoric,*
trans. E. CAMPBELL and J. COLTON (New York: Appleton-Century-Crofts, 1960),
II, 212-214; cf. George SARTON, *Introduction to the History of Science,* II, ii, 655.

[10] On the death of Palinurus, who fell asleep at the helm and pitched overboard,
see VERGIL's *Aeneid,* V, 854 ff.

[11] Cf. the shipwreck scene in the *Aeneid,* I, 102 ff.

waters,"[12] to keep afloat that which he has redeemed from his enemies at such great price! Otherwise I fear greatly that we may be driven by the storm to perish either at the hands of pirates or on the rocky shore.

This is where we have been brought by our helmsman's foolishness — I am too generous: his blindness. The description is justified. One should speak accurately, and choose the right words for things. Rage, madness, shameful sloth, burning desire for the stormy shore, reason's realm abandoned to Fortune, the disreputable grossness which comes from the urging of foul greed[13] — these are what have done it. Alas, how much more fortunate it would have been if he had furrowed the earth with his father's plough rather than boarded the fisherman's craft. What am I to say? I am certainly aware that a specific remedy[14] will not cure a universal disease. But what more is to be done? And so he goes to receive his deserts, a feast for the sharks, pointed to by all, the butt of their wit, a universal joke, the jest of dinner tables — in a word, a fable forever for all who sail these waters.

But what of us, do you think? Surely, if the same kind of captain takes over the helm, the goddess Safety herself will hardly be able to save us, even if she wants to.[15] Our only hope of salvation in such terrible circumstances is that no such portent exists. But look about you to see if there

---

[12] *Ibid.*, V, 867-868.
[13] It is hard to know whether this refers to the swelling of Clement's head and face when he was ill in 1351, or the well-known corpulence of Benedict XII who is described by the hostile Gualvaneus de la Flamma as "swollen of neck and limbs, a hearty eater and a heavy drinker" (*Opusculum de rebus gestis,* ed C. CASTIGLIONI, in MURATORI, *Scriptores rerum italicarum,* XII, iv, 15).
[14] The death of the incumbent pope, which Petrarch seems to expect at any moment.
[15] See PLAUTUS, *Captivi,* III, iii, 14.

is some plank to which we might together cling and so swim to dry land.[16] If you ask me, we shall be best off remaining in your rural retreat,[17] granted that such be possible. There, it seems to me, is the hoped-for peace and the calmest harbour.

Think on this, and farewell.

2

The next three letters have to do with Cola di Rienzo. Letters 2 and 3 were sent to Cola in 1347, when he was in command of Rome. Letter 4 was addressed to the Roman people in 1352, on behalf of Cola who was now imprisoned in Avignon awaiting trial. But Petrarch's subject in these letters was not simply Cola. He wrote of Rome, Italy and revenge: of Rome slowly recovering her lost vitality, about to take up again that rule of the world so unjustly usurped by barbarians, of Italy united and at peace, and of revenge for the contempt in which Italy and Italians had been held at the papal court.

Cola di Rienzo was born in 1313. He was a well-educated notary in Rome, with a strong antiquarian interest in Roman history and historical monuments. He came to political prominence in 1343 when, as a result of a popular uprising, the control of the usually ungovernable city was placed in the hands of a council of heads of various merchant guilds. At this time there was a delegation of Romans in Avignon pleading with the pope, Clement VI, that he accept the by now nominal position of Senator of Rome for life, return the papal court to the city, and designate the year 1350 as a jubilee year on the model of the jubilee of 1300 granted by Boniface VIII. The revolutionary coun-

---

[16] See CICERO, *De officiis*, III, 23, 89.
[17] Vaucluse.

cil in Rome now sent an additional delegate, Cola, whose purpose it was to give the pope a true picture of the miserable conditions of Rome. He proceeded to antagonize many in Avignon with his outspoken attacks on those responsible for Rome's turmoil, the great noble families. He especially upset Cardinal Giovanni Colonna, a member of one of those families. Despite his loyalty to the cardinal, Petrarch was immensely stirred by Cola's vision of a Rome at peace, an Italy unified, and the old Roman empire reborn. He did everything he could to dispel the cardinal's suspicions, and through him he succeeded in obtaining from the pope the formal appointment of Cola as notary to the government of Rome.

Cola returned to Rome in 1344. On May 20, 1347, during the absence of the senators and much of the nobility from the city, he led a revolution, and in the presence of a popular gathering on the Capitoline he proclaimed a new constitution. Soon after, he acclaimed himself tribune with dictatorial powers.

When Petrarch heard of all this in early June he was tremendously enthusiastic, as one can tell from the following two letters, in spite of his close connection with the Colonna family. He quickly shot off a warm and laudatory letter to Cola and the Roman people (he did not include it in his published correspondence), an essay on freedom which treated Cola as the liberator of his people. Meanwhile, events moved swiftly in Rome. Cola forced the nobles to accept his new constitution and for a while it seemed that he might put an end to the continual civil war which plagued the unhappy city. But as the summer went on there were alarming signs of megalomania. Cola took for himself grandiose titles, indulged in exaggerated displays of costume, excessive pomp and strange ceremonies, and went so far as to bathe in the baptismal font at St. John Lateran in which, as tradition had it, the emperor Constantine the Great had been baptized by Pope Sylvester and so cured of leprosy. He demanded the submission of all the rulers of the world of whatever rank or dignity to Rome as the head of the universe. His increasing wildness soured the papal vicar in Rome, whom Cola shunted aside, and the early favour of the papacy now turned to hostility. In Rome, popular enthusiasm for the re- volution also cooled. When the nobility took up arms late in the year Cola found himself without support. He had been curiously ineffective when he had had his enemies within his power, humiliating them but generally shying away from violence; as a result his enemies multiplied, his supporters lost faith, and he himself became a nervous wreck, suffering nightmares. When, therefore, the counter-revolution came on December 15, he ran away.

All that year Petrarch had written encouraging letters to Cola; but the extremes of the last few months had disillusioned him, as they had many others, and his last letter to Cola, written on November 29, 1347, was a letter of reprimand (and therefore the only letter to Cola that he *would* include in his published correspondence) calling on him to exercise a certain amount of self-examination and criticism, quite a change in tone from the following.

Your Excellency's courier will tell you from his own experience what kind of humanity, mercy or justice you might hope to find here! A new kind of cruelty, this, that an unaccompanied, unwary and innocent lad should be attacked as though he were an enemy; that both the rod[1] (which, if they had any sense here, they should have feared and respected), as well as the dispatch-case filled with the most serious and gracious letters, should be dashed to pieces on his undeserving head! That those letters, which might have softened hearts made of marble, should be torn up and scattered! What hospitality! What charity! Your courier, who was seized at the Durance river, tortured, beaten, forbidden entry into the city, and packed off with threats to go with his bruises and wounds, has gone back to bow his bleeding head at your feet.

Durance indeed! So you are called in the vernacular, from

---

[1] Petrarch uses the word *virga*. In ancient Rome the lictor's *fasces*, a bundle of rods, was a magisterial symbol. Apparently the young messenger was carrying some such symbol when he was set upon.

the harshness of your wines[2] — or Ruance, as some writers
refer to you, from the verb "to rush".[3] Oh swift, destructive
river, the inhabitants along your banks are no kinder than
your rapids and rough bed, and rush into every kind of crime
with just as much fury. Oh you streams so shamelessly proud,
so irreverent and faithless: you river Sorgues, sucking in what is
not your own and swelling up proudly against your lord; you
Rhone, gnawing at everything! Is this the way you recognize
the Tiber? Is this the way you honour your master?

Oh Avignon, whose vineyard, if we may believe the prophets,
will bring forth bitter grapes and a bloody vintage, is this the
way you honour your mistress Rome? Is this being mindful
of your servitude and her high station? Heaven help you if
she begins to arouse herself, and especially if she raises her
head and sees the hurts and injuries done to her whilst she
slept. For she is now awake, believe me; she sleeps no more,
but only remains silent, and in her silence dreams again of
times gone by, planning what she will do when she rises.
Wait a brief moment; you will see great events in the world,
and you will be amazed that what you would have earlier
thought impossible is now happening. Are you not forgetting
what you are, where you are, and to whom you are subject?
Do you not know the origins of the name "Provence"? What
wild madness is this? Has forgetfulness of all storms crept
over you because of some passing calm? Is this the way you
revere the mistress of the provinces? She slept; you believed
her dead, and like a slavegirl set free by the death of her mistress,
you thought yourself a slave still unless you proved your

---

[2] *Durities antium>Durentia* (Durance). Etymological exercises of this kind were
very common in the Middle Ages.
[3] *Ruo, ruere.*

freedom by your iniquities. You want to be considered important and powerful. For some time in our foolishness we allowed your wish to be fulfilled; we warn you now, the time has come to return to your senses. There are many whose power does not come from their own strength, but from the weakness of others; their power surely declines as that of the opponent revives. You will know what you are when you have come to recognize what Rome is still, whose agents you have so insulted just now thinking that there is no one to avenge them. You are wrong, foolish, mad. There is someone in heaven who will avenge them, God; and there is someone here who will avenge them, a friend of God whom you do not know.[4] There are forces abroad the very existence of which you cannot even suspect. Ah, you wretch, you will find out — soon, I hope. The wrongs you have done us[5] have given us back our strength. From the moment we first began to suffer we took a great stride forward to health and vigour.

But you, illustrious sir, have mercy upon our affairs. Rouse up our burgeoning homeland and show the unbelieving heathen how powerful Rome now is. As for the rest of Italy, who can doubt that she is as strong as she ever was, wanting neither wisdom nor vigour, neither riches nor courage, but only a common will? Once she has that, then to those who joke about Italy's name I hereby announce by the tenor of this present letter a slaughter and destruction soon to come. You, I say, whom the fates have chosen to take the lead in such great matters, press on with what you have started. You have nothing to fear. These petty clouds will fade away before the radiant sun; the shrewdness of little foxes will not with-

[4] Presumably Cola.
[5] Romans or Italians.

stand the attack of the lion.[6] You have begun in glory. Go on
bravely and persevere to the end. Show Pride how much
lower it is than Humility, and Greed how much poorer it is
than Generosity; show Fraud how stupid it is when set before
Prudence, and Lust how shameful it is when compared with
Temperance and Decency. Now at last let hypocritical Deceit
know what a nothing it is where true Virtue shines.

Act now. Do not delay. Trample, grind, crush the frog
foolishly puffed up to resemble a great ox. I do not speak
to urge you. You do not need anyone to push you forward
or hold you back. You have your own spur and bridle. But I
have been unable to bear my heart's grief in silence. My
pain, swollen by speaking of it, has swelled my complaint,
and as my words have fed my anger, so my anger has fed my
words. For who may look unmoved upon the fact that the
law of nations has been violated and the covenant of human-
kind rejected in the violation and rejection of the person of
your messenger.

What anger, to be so unmindful of honour! Your courier
would have been better off among barbarian enemies than
among those whom you thought were civilized Latins, whose
good will you deserved. If there are any left among them who
can recognize riches other than the kind they are usually
greedy for, let them examine history. Let them look into the
past and then answer me this: what barbarian, except very
rarely, ever abused emissaries, especially for no cause? The
treacherous, faithless Carthaginian mob tried this once with
our legates, but their violence was stopped when the magistrates

---

[6] This seems to be a reference to the little foxes that spoil the vine (Song of
Solomon, 2, 15). The equation between vine and Avignon (*vinea, Avinio*) has
already been made in the letter.

intervened.[7] Now who, I ask, stopped the violence in this case? Who handed down punishment for it? But I am too severe — who even complained of it or deplored it? How much safer your courier would have been in going to Parthia when Crassus and his son were beheaded and our legions routed; how much more secure he would have been going to Germany when the Teutons were slaughtered and Marius triumphed, than he was in coming here on behalf of you who venerate the Roman church as a son? Surely neither the insolence of the Parthian victor nor the bitterness of the conquered German enemy would have dared as much as did the envy of this false friendship. Your lad might have more easily crossed the tree-covered mountain of Pelion and the frigid Taurus range in mid-winter than the plain of Orgon[8] on a mild autumn day, or have swum the Ganges and the Ebro with less difficulty than the Durance.

I had to say all this to get it out of my system. But as for you, noble sir, do not be deterred by injury or by the workers of injury, and certainly not by their false appearance of greatness. The power to hurt is no sign of true greatness or of true strength; it is the mark of the meanest and weakest creatures. True greatness is the power to help, and truer greatness is the will to help. The wickedest men have been able to injure an innocent boy, and to have replied thus to your message. What is great about that? Rather, is it not less than nothing? For if all sin is nothing, the greater the

---

[7] Livy, XXX, xxv, 2-3; see Petrarch's *Africa,* VI, 789-794 (ed. Nicola Festa, Florence, 1926, p. 164).

[8] A town on the south bank of the Durance where the attack presumably took place.

sin the greater its nothingness.[9] So the greatness of sin, if "greatness" be the word, amounts to nothing. It is with this kind of greatness that these mighty fellows have now exercised their talents. They did what a scorpion, a spider, might have done. They injured one of your servants, and (what this terrible offence makes even more obvious) they hoped to injure you — not simply you as yourself, but you as the guardian of liberty and justice. For they hate you only because of these ideals, and these they hate because of their nature — because in them they recognize a threat to their unjust exercise of authority in which they take so much pride. If you will but consult the greatness of your own spirit, you will at once despise and scorn their vanity and empty purpose.

These are matters sharp and painful, but they are really petty. Matters of greater moment are at stake. These little things, like everything else, will pass, and your servant will finally be avenged when the Republic has been avenged.

Farewell, and finish what you have started.

3

The matter that now weighs down my spirits is a trifle. Still, I must vomit it up, for to neglect it will harm my stomach. It is not its size that upsets me; even though small, it brings on an immense nausea. Indeed, it reeks of the hidden poison of an old, deep hatred. So it has seemed to me; so it will seem, I am sure, to you; and should it become more widely

---

[9] See St. Augustine's commentary on the gospel of St. John (I, i, 13) in MIGNE, *Patrologia Latina,* XXXV, 1385: "...quia peccatum nihil est, et nihil fiunt homines cum peccant."

known, I hope that it will thrust the sting of righteous indignation into the souls of all the people of Rome and of Italy, and drive out the heavy inertia which keeps the old, noble-natured power dormant. Once the whole world bowed to that power, by compulsion or by choice; today, alas, the vilest of men mock at it. Should it rise again, as I hope, it will not be a bad thing for the Republic. A little spark has often started a great fire; a single word has often led to many great results. But now the matter itself must be dealt with, nor should it be magnified by my words as much as by the anger of those who read them.

Well then, not long ago, among some of those people who think themselves so smart (though others perhaps do not think so), a formal debate was held on the question: "would it not be best for the world if the city of Rome and Italy were united and at peace?"[1] And although to doubt the matter was itself childish and silly enough, still it might have been excused because of their zeal in debating everything under the sun, except that after many arguments had been tossed back and forth, he who was considered the wisest of the lot delivered the venomous decision: "it would be of no benefit whatever," with the approval and applause of all!

Most eloquent sir, would you, I beg, inform the Roman populace of what I have said when you next orate in public as is your custom, so that they may know the sentiments of these high and mighty people respecting our welfare.

---

[1] This was no discussion of "the cardinals in consistory" as Wilkins has it (*Life of Petrarch*, p. 70) or a "conference of high prelates" (Bishop, *Petrarch and his World*, p. 263). It is the old formal disputation of the university world cast in the form of a *questio*. Apparently it was a common intellectual exercise in Avignon, to which Petrarch refers elsewhere. He mentions in the next sentence the great zeal for such debates in Avignon.

Even if they do no harm with their opinions, nevertheless they reveal their true colours by their windy talk, whilst what they want for us they want so desperately that they cannot hide it, and in their foul blindness try to substitute their iniquitous desire and hateful design for reason. But they will die in their error; we are in the hands of God, and shall not suffer the fate they hope for us, but enjoy that which God has prepared for us.

I was not present at these ravings. I might have upset some of them there, for silence would have been neither honourable nor, for me, possible in the midst of such impious talk. Further, when the matter was reported to me I was outraged, and upheld the contrary view among our friends; as little as my authority may be, I uphold it now with you, lord of our liberty. As a petitioner, by all the angels in heaven, I beg you especially, and also the Roman people and all Italy that you will confirm by your deeds what I maintain with my words. I hope that you may live long in prosperous condition, and rule successfully over the Republic which you have bravely liberated.

4

After some wandering, Cola turned up in Prague looking for the support of the emperor Charles IV. Charles sent him to Avignon as a prisoner in 1352. There he remained, chained up in a tower reading Pope Clement's copy of Livy, until a new pope, Innocent VI, decided to use him to restore Rome to papal loyalty. He was released in September 1353; he turned up in Rome in July 1354, and was made a senator. Almost immediately he returned to the kind of disturbing behaviour that had discouraged his followers seven years earlier, swinging wildly from deep depression to exhuberant gaiety. He quickly lost all public support and was killed and beheaded by a mob on October 9, 1354.

Letter 4 was written to the people of the city of Rome around October-November 1352, while Cola was still a prisoner in Avignon. The burden of the letter is clear enough. While there is some trivial criticism of Cola it is more than offset by the large admiration that Petrarch has for Cola's accomplishments and his respect for and support of Cola's ideas, especially the notion that the centre of the Roman empire remains in the city of Rome, and that its authority rightly rests in Roman hands.

When Cola was brought to Avignon in July 1352, one of his first questions had been whether Petrarch was there. In fact, Petrarch was in Vaucluse all that summer. While we have no direct evidence that the two men saw one another before Petrarch left Provence for the last time in May 1353, it is difficult to believe that they did not, and there are one or two indications in the following letter that Petrarch saw and talked with Cola or at least had direct reports on, and several conversations about, his condition and his opinions.

Before you, my own invincible people, conquerors of nations, before you I must bring an important and widely-known affair. I ask and beg of you, noble sirs, to give me your attention. It is a matter of great importance to you — indeed, of the greatest importance; there is nothing in the world to match it. But in case I should wear out the patience of those of you eager to learn more about it, or try to magnify with words what is already by its very nature of the greatest magnitude, I leave aside all introductory comments and come to the business itself.

What an unhappy sight! Your former tribune, now held captive in a foreign land like a thief in the night or a traitor to his homeland, pleads his case while in chains. He has been denied that right of self-defence which judges and magistrates of justice throughout the world have never rightly refused even to one accused of sacrilege. Perhaps he deserves to be treated in this way, for deserting, at the very moment of its flowering, the Roman Republic which was established by his own genius — which was planted, so to speak, by his own hands, and then took root and bloomed. But Rome does not deserve such treatment. Her citizens used to be protected by the law, and were exempt from punishment, but everywhere now they are oppressed by the cruel decision of this person or that as though such were no crime but rather a virtue to be loudly applauded.

In order that you may know, illustrious sirs, about the charge laid against your one-time head and ruler — or should I now call him your fellow-citizen or your exile — you will now hear something which, whether known to you or not, is certainly astonishing and shameful. He is charged not with neglecting, if you please, but with defending liberty. He stands accused not of deserting but of occupying the Capitol. And the worst charge flung at him, deserving of the death penalty, is that he dared to claim that the Roman empire was still in Rome and belonged to the Roman people.

What an impious age we live in! What savage envy and unheard-of malevolence! What are you doing, oh Christ, infallible and perfect judge? Where are your eyes with which you usually dispel the shadows of human misery? Why do you turn them away? Why do they not flash out twin balls of fire to destroy this shameful trial? "Look down on us and have mercy" (Ps. 118, 132), even though we do not deserve it. "Consider our enemies," who are no less your own; "they are many and they hate us with a cruel hatred" (Ps. 24, 19), and hate you no less. Distinguish, we beseech you, between parties so utterly different. "Then may our sentence come forth from your presence; then may your eyes behold equity" (Ps. 16, 2).

Surely we need be neither angered nor surprised that any nation — indeed, every nation, as we know — submitted only unwillingly to the Roman yoke, though it was the least unjust or galling of any. For there is in the spirits of mortals a deep-seated yearning after liberty, often ill-advised and hasty; and often, too, since a sense of ignominy keeps one from obeying one's betters, those who might be good subjects make bad rulers. Thus everything is mixed up and confused, which is why we sometimes see fawning servitude where there should be noble rule, unjust rule where there should be a proper servitude. If things were only otherwise, human affairs would be in better shape and the world would be more virtuous, its leadership still unimpaired. If you do not believe me, then put your trust in the evidence of the past. When was there ever such peace, such tranquillity and such justice; when was virtue so honoured, the good so rewarded and the evil punished; when was there ever such wise direction of affairs, than when the world had only one head and that head was Rome? Better still, at what time did God, the lover of peace and justice, choose to be born of the Virgin and visit the earth?

Each body has been given one head. The universe, described by the poet as a great body,[1] ought then to be content with a single earthly head, for every two-headed animal is a monster.[2] How much more frightful and monstrous is the creature with a thousand different heads, all gnawing at and struggling against each other! Even allowing that there may be several heads, there still has to be one, surely, to restrain all the others and to preside over them in order that the peace of

---

[1] *Aeneid*, VI, 727.
[2] The metaphor is a commonplace in the writings of medieval political thinkers.

the entire body remain indisturbed. Indeed, we have learned
from long experience and on the authority of the most
learned men that, as in heaven so on earth, a single ruler
has always been best. Omnipotent God has declared by many
signs that he wished the supreme head to be none other
than Rome, which he has made worthy by glory in war and
by great preeminence as a nation of remarkable and unex-
ampled virtue.

All the same, it must be allowed that a nation may be
excused on grounds of carelessness or stupidity if, like people
who daily rejoice in their own misfortune, it chooses to
embrace what I have called a pernicious and specious liberty
rather than the safe and sound rule of the mother of nations.
But who may hear, without being upset, the question being
debated among these learned fellows, whether the Roman
empire be in Rome? With the kingdoms of the Parthians,
Persians and Medes located among the Parthians, Persians
and Medes, are we then to believe that the empire of the
Romans will wander around? Who can stomach such vile
stuff? Who would not rather heave it up from the very pit
of his being? If the Roman empire is not in Rome then
where, I ask, is it? Obviously, if it is somewhere else than
in Rome, then it is no longer an empire of Romans but
rather of those to whom changeable Fortune has granted an
empire. For even though the Roman emperors, for the good
of the state, often led their armies to the farthest east or
west, to north or south, the Roman empire meanwhile stayed
in Rome. It was Rome that decided which of the Roman
emperors deserved reward or punishment. It was on the
Capitol that they decided who was to be honoured, who
punished; whether on entering the city one was to be denied
public recognition, or was to be honoured with an ovation

or a triumph. Indeed, after Julius Caesar's rule, whether we prefer to call it a tyranny or a monarchy, the Roman emperors, though now enrolled among the gods, still had to seek permission from the Senate or people of Rome for what they did, and on the grant or denial of that permission depended whether they could do what they proposed or not. Emperors, therefore, may go here and there, but the empire is always fixed in the same place. Vergil was not speaking of some short-lived kingdom, but of an eternal empire, when he wrote the words: "while the race of Aeneas shall live by the steadfast rock of the Capitol, and Rome's lord shall hold sway."[3] For these words promised glory to those two,[4] not for a hundred years or a thousand, but for all time.

In case anyone thinks that all this is mere flattery, fit neither for my tongue nor for your ears, let me here digress. I know that in this matter Vergil received a not unjust reprimand somewhere in Augustine, and then soon after in the same work he was most justly pardoned. Where Vergil has Jove speak of you, the Roman people, he writes: "Romulus shall take the people under his protection and build the Martian walls; he shall call them Romans from his own name." He then adds to this tale of the city's origin a comment on its unbroken future: "I impose on them no limit of space or of time; I have given them an empire without end."[5]

---

[3] *Aeneid*, IX, 448-449.

[4] Nisus and Euryalus, followers of Aeneas. Vergil promises that their brave exploits and death will never be lost to memory as long as Rome stands; *Aeneid*, IX, 446-449.

[5] *Ibid.*, I, 276-9. On the idea of an eternal Rome, which had its first expression in the late first century B.C., see F.G. MOORE, "On Urbs Aeterna and Urbs Sacra," *Transactions of the American Philological Association*. XXV (1894), 34-60, and Kenneth J. PRATT, "Rome as Eternal," *Journal of the History of Ideas*, XXVI (1965), 25-44.

Augustine says, and quite properly: How will he give an "empire without end" who has never given, nor has been able to give, anything more than what might be given by any sinful mortal who is burdened and oppressed, rather than adorned, by a false reputation of divinity?

But leave this aside, for whoever bestowed the Roman empire — and it was surely none other than omnipotent God, who alone rules heaven and earth, from whom all empires come — the question that Augustine asks is this: Where is the empire located, "on earth or in heaven? Surely," he continues, "on earth. Even if it were in heaven, both heaven and earth will pass away.[6] If what God himself made will pass away, then how much more swiftly what Romulus founded!"[7]

So Augustine on Vergil. It is certainly clear that all kingdoms, and whatever anywhere appears illustrious or magnificent in our eyes, if not already in ruins will at all events come crashing down in the future when God who created them shakes heaven and earth. "He will make a new heaven and a new earth" (Apoc. 21, 1), nor will he lie like Jupiter, for "he is the truth" (John, 14, 6). That kingdom is his which has no beginning and will have no end, of which it is written: "and of his kingdom there shall be no end" (Luke, 1, 33).

As it happens, this was unknown to Vergil on whom almighty God lavished genius and eloquence and yet denied those things "hidden from the wise and revealed to the meek" (Matt., 11, 25); but he was certainly not ignorant

---

[6] MATT., 24, 35; MARK, 13, 31; LUKE, 21, 33.
[7] Petrarch is quoting a sermon of Augustine's (no. 105, cap. 7, para. 10, in MIGNE, *Patrologia Latina*, XXXVIII, 622-3).

of the fact that all kingdoms which had had a beginning would ultimately perish. But he was very careful. Where he promised immortality to the Roman empire he did not speak in his own person, but put the words into Jove's mouth, so that the fraudulent oracle and false promise would be that of a lying god. To flatter the Roman people he used someone else to lie. But elsewhere, when he wished to speak in his own person, the poet did not hide the truth, but referred to "the Roman state and realms destined to perish."[8] How can one miss the obvious difference between "an empire without end" and "realms destined to perish?" But the first is out of the mouth of Jupiter, the false god; the second that of Vergil, the man of genius. Though in somewhat different words, it was certainly from this point of view that Augustine first accused and then excused Vergil. What I have already said, and what I shall say further, is based on the same point of view.

Furthermore, it was a Roman who said "everything that is born must die; all things that grow, grow old."[9] In time, therefore, all things grow old. Indeed, if the end of anything is its old age, then everything not already senile is certainly becoming so: for everything upright eventually falls and the fall is either preceded or at least accompanied by old age. There is no exception; whether they last long or not, all growing things sooner or later decline and waste away. Inconstant Fortune will turn her wheel ceaselessly, and will toss transient kingdoms from one people to another. In her wilfulness she will fashion kings out of slaves and slaves out of kings. She will wield her irresistible power over the city of Rome and the Roman world. You especially, noble

[8] *Geor.* II, 498.
[9] SALLUST, *Jug.* II, 3.

sirs, she has long oppressed in the most trying ways, and
is still doing so. Perhaps many have pitied you, though no
one has given you much help. I know this; I grieve; I am
angered more than one can believe; but I am powerless to
do more.

Not that I am troubled because Fortune is as wayward with
you as with others, and that in order to prove herself un-
disputed mistress of human affairs she does not hesitate to lay
rude hands on the very head of those affairs. I know her harshness. I have suffered her unpredictable ways. But I can hardly
tolerate the empty boasting of certain subject tribes who now
proudly arch necks still calloused from Rome's yoke.

And so, not to mention many other unhappy matters,
the question is now debated[10] — sad and shameful tale —
whether the Roman empire is at Rome. Agreed, where now
there is a wild forest a royal palace may some day rise, and
where now there are halls resplendent with the glow of gold
hungry flocks may later graze and the wandering shepherd
may dwell in the private chambers of kings. I do not under-
estimate Fortune's power. She can cast down utterly the
queen of cities as she has other cities, and with no greater
effort wreak on her even greater ruin. Sad to say, she has
almost done just that. But what she will certainly never be
able to bring about is the establishment of the Roman empire in any other place than Rome, for as soon as it is
found elsewhere it will cease to be Roman.

Your unhappy fellow-citizen does not deny that he held
these views or holds them now. This is the great crime that
has brought him to the brink of death. He adds that he
has maintained these views on the authority of many wise

---

10 Another *questio*, the subject of which must have infuriated Petrarch.

persons, nor do I think he lies. He begs to be given the opportunity to make his defence and to be given an advocate. He is refused. Unless divine mercy and your support come to his rescue, he is done for. Innocent and defenceless as he is, he will be condemned. Many men feel sympathy for him. There is almost no one (outside the ranks of those whose responsibility it was to pity and forgive transgressions, not envy virtues)[11] who does not feel sorry for him. Furthermore, there are some outstanding jurists here who say that his claim clearly can be supported from civil law. There are some who say that they can find much valid evidence to substantiate his point of view in the annals of the past, if only one might be free to speak out. But there is no one who dares even whisper except in corners, in the shadows, in fear.

I myself, who write you this letter and who might not refuse to die for the truth if my death would do anything for the state, remain silent; nor do I put my name to this letter, feeling that its style alone is sufficient to identify me. Let me add, however, that I am a Roman citizen.[12] But if the case were being heard in a safe place before an impartial judge, and not in the court of our enemies, I think I might — the truth illuminating my soul and God guiding my tongue or pen — say a few words which could throw a clearer light on the fact that the Roman empire, though now wasted and long oppressed by the buffets of Fortune, and occupied at different times by Spaniards, Africans, Greeks, Gauls and Germans, still, as diminished as it is, remains in Rome and

---

[11] The clergy in Avignon.
[12] He became a Roman citizen in 1341 on the occasion of his coronation with the laurel wreath.

nowhere else. There it will stay though there be nothing left of that mighty city but the bare rock of the Capitol. I would say further that before we were subjected to foreign control and only the Roman Caesars ruled, all rights of empire were vested not in the emperors but in the Senate and people of Rome, if it is true in law that one who possesses a thing in bad faith at no time may acquire a prescriptive right.[13]

In the present situation, while time drags on (a gift from on high, perhaps, by which this great matter may yet see the light of day, something which until now you hardly dared hope for), I could not overlook the one thing which touched you and the dignity of Rome's name. I was compelled to reach for my pen by that faith by which I embrace you and your city above all others in special love and veneration. I urge and beg you not to desert your fellow-citizen, who has been placed in such jeopardy, but have your ambassadors claim him by showing that he is one of you. For even though they try to snatch the imperial title from you, they are not yet so mad that they dare deny you jurisdiction over your own citizens. Surely, if he committed an offence he did so at Rome. There can be no doubt that jurisdiction for offences committed in Rome belongs to you, unless you are now to be denied a common right of law, you who founded the law, developed it, and transmitted it to other nations. For where more justly may you punish crimes than where they were committed, and where the place itself, by reminding the guilty of their shameful offence, plays a not insignificant part in their punishment, and witnessing the penalty either reassures or terrifies those who witness the crime? But if by chance your tribune deserves to be rewarded rather than

---

[13] *Digest,* 41, 2, 1, para. 6. I owe this reference to Rev. L.E. Boyle, O.P.

punished — as many, indeed all good men feel — where better might he receive his reward than where he earned it? Nowhere is the reward of a brave man more deservedly bestowed than where he acted bravely, so that those who saw the deed will be inspired by the reward to imitate it. So claim your fellow-citizen with confidence; you are asking for nothing new, nothing unjust — rather, you will do wrong if you remain silent.

But if it is claimed that by the law of "common country" he should be punished where he is presently held captive, how much more truly in his case is Rome the "common country," where he was born and raised, and where he did whatever it was that he is accused of? Here,[14] on the contrary, he has done nothing to be either praised or blamed. If, however, unlike your forefathers, your courage has declined with your fortune, and has so degenerated that to demand justice seems rash to you whose forefathers found nothing difficult, then at least ask for what can be asked of any barbaric nation living under law, namely that your fellow-citizen not be denied a public hearing and the right to make his lawful defence, so that he who did everything out in the light of day, and indeed shed on the world as much light as any man could, may not be condemned in darkness.

Finally, show that you are not indifferent to the trial, to the fate, of your fellow-citizen. Stand firm against injustice. Prevent wrong. Protect the accused if innocent, judge him if guilty. At the very least, stop him from being judged at just anyone's whim. Bring as much help as you can and ought to your tribune — or if that title has lost its effect, your fellow-citizen. He deserves much from the state,

---

[14] In Avignon, where Cola is being held.

especially because he revived a great question of importance
to the world,[15] which for many centuries lay asleep and
buried: it is the one way to the restitution of public order
and the beginning of a golden age. Help him. Do not neglect
his safety, for he exposed himself to a thousand dangers and
undying hatred for yours. Think about his aims and ideas;
remember in what condition your affairs had been, and how
suddenly, with the help and by the effort of this one man,
to what heights of hope not only Rome but all Italy soared,
how great the Italian name suddenly became, how renewed
and refurbished the glory of Rome, how great the fear and
grief of our enemies, the joy of our friends, the expectations of
our people; how changed the direction of events, how changed
the face of the earth, how different the desires of people, how
nothing under heaven seemed the same. What a remarkable
and sudden transformation that was! He held the reins of
government for no more than seven months,[16] and in such a
way, I believe, that hardly anything greater than this has been
tried since the beginning of time. If he had brought to
completion what he had begun, it would have seemed . a
divine rather than a human achievement. Indeed, whatever
is well done by man is a divine achievement. To him, therefore, who as we know exerted himself for your glory rather
than his own ambition, you surely owe much. Fortune must
be held responsible for what happened afterwards. If any
slackening followed the initial enthusiasm, blame the foolish
waywardness of men, and liberate while you still can your
fellow-citizen from injustice, just as, despite the great danger,
you freed the Greeks from the injustices of the Macedonians,

---

[15] Because of him we can debate a *questio* of real importance: the superior place
of Rome in the world.
[16] May-December, 1347.

the Sicilians from the Carthaginians, the Campanians from the Samnites, the Etruscans from the Gauls. I know that you have few resources; but your ancestors never had more spirit than when Roman poverty flourished and they were rich only in virtue. I am also aware that your strength has declined; believe me, if there is a drop of the old blood still in your veins, then your grandeur is far from slight, your authority far from insignificant. Dare something, I beg you, in memory of the Roman state, in memory of the ashes and the glory of your forefathers, in the name of the empire, and in the mercy of Jesus Christ who orders us to love our neighbours and to succour the weak. Dare something, I beg you, especially since to speak out is honourable while silence is dishonourable and shameful. Dare something, if not for his safety, then for your own honour. Dare something if you want to be something.[17] Nothing is less Roman than fear. I warn you, moreover, that if you are afraid, if you despise yourself, then there will be many others to despise you too and no one to fear you; but if you start now to resist the scorn of others, you will be feared far and wide, as often happened of old and happened again more recently when he of whom I speak governed Rome. Only speak with a single voice and let the world know that it is the united voice of the Roman people. No one will ever ridicule or despise that voice; everyone will respect it or fear it. Reclaim now this prisoner, or insist on justice. One or the other demand will be granted. You who once freed the king of Egypt from a siege of the Syrians with a small legation, free now your fellow-citizen from this undeserved imprisonment.

---

[17] JUVENAL, *Sat.* I, 73-74.

5

On April 1, 1352, Petrarch wrote a letter to Lapo da Castiglion-chio of Florence which he would later include in his large collection of *Familiares*. The first part of the letter, however, was too biting in its criticism of the papacy to be made public, so Petrarch separated it from the rest and placed it in the *Liber sine nomine* as the following selection, as though it were complete in itself.

Lapo was one of a small number of Petrarch's enthusiastic admirers in Florence, which included Giovanni Boccaccio and Francesco Nelli — a kind of Florentine fan club. It was Petrarch's knowledge and authority as a classicist that they marvelled at, and all were as keen as he was about the discovery and sharing of the works of ancient authors. Lapo sent Petrarch some orations of Cicero in 1349, and the following year, when Petrarch visited Florence after being in Rome for the jubilee, also gave him his copy of Quintilian's *Institutes*. Though Lapo would follow a legal career, he maintained a strong interest in Petrarch's work. When he was expelled from Florence in 1378, the year of the Ciompi revolt, he visited Padua where he assiduously searched out and copied as many of the master's works as he could find.

I have a two-fold Parnassus, the one in Italy,[1] the other among the Gauls[2] — a sort of double temple for the far-wandering Muses. I was happier on the Italian Helicon "while fate and God allowed" as that unhappy lover says in Vergil[3] — if indeed Dido really was an unhappy lover and not a most chaste and faithful woman. Now the Gallic world holds me, and the western Babylon (than which the sun shines on nothing more deformed), and the savage Rhone, so like hell's boiling Cocytus or Acheron. Here are enthroned

---

[1] His house at Selvapiana near Parma.
[2] His home at Vaucluse; see *Fam.* V, 10, in Rossi II, 30.
[3] *Aeneid,* IV, 651.

the heirs of the fishermen[4] — once poor, now remarkably
forgetful of their origins. It is astonishing to recall those
earlier ones, and then to look upon their successors covered
with gold and purple, made proud with the spoils of princes
and nations — to see luxurious palaces in place of the overturned boats, to see mountain-girdling walls instead of the
little nets with which so long ago on the billowing waves of
the Galilean lake they sought with much difficulty a bare
living, and with which on the Lake of Gennesaret they toiled
all night and took nothing (though when morning came they
took a huge number of fishes in the name of Jesus). It is
shocking to hear now the lying tongues, to see the parchments
devoid of truth turned by their dangling seals into nets to
entangle a credulous host of Christians — also in the name
of Jesus, but for the works of Belial. They are soon scaled,
cooked in the flames of cares and the "coals of desolation"
(Ps. 119, 2-4), and go to fill the pit of a greedy belly. It is shocking
to see pious solitude replaced with shameful comings and
goings and swarming troupes of the most debased hangers-on,
to see rich feasts in place of sober fasts, rude and revolting
slothfulness for sacred pilgrimages — and instead of the naked
feet of the apostles, to gaze upon the prancing snow-white
mounts of thieves, bedecked with gold, covered with gold,
champing on gold bits, soon to be shod with gold shoes if
the Lord does not curtail this debased excess. What more?
You might think that they are the kings of the Persians or the
Parthians, to be adored, whom it would be criminal to greet
without offering a gift. You poor, worn ancients![5] For what

---

[4] The cardinals, often likened to the apostles.
[5] The apostles.

did you toil? For what purpose did you sow in the Lord's field? To what end did you shed your sacred blood to nourish the crop? But I cannot go on.

Pity now the evil fate that has befallen your friend in this place. He certainly does not deserve this punishment, though he might some other. Here I am now, an old man, dragged by Fate (though I thought myself free) back here where I once spent my childhood, to a distasteful childishness once more. And here I am so used up, so worn out, and so exhausted that as my sickness of soul has now slowly affected my body I am sick all over, and can talk of nothing but unrelieved complaints and grudges. So I have had to put off many things which were on my mind. My whole stomach is giving me trouble, so you should not hope for anything gentle from me today. You cannot get fresh water from a brackish well. It is natural that the breath from an ulcered breast be offensive, the words of a wounded soul bitter.

6

This letter was written on March 31, 1352, to Francesco Nelli. He was a priest in Florence, Prior of the Church of the Holy Apostles, and secretary to the bishop Angelo Acciaiuoli, another friend of Petrarch. He was one of that small band of Petrarchan enthusiasts in Florence that included Lapo da Castiglionchio, the recipient of letter 5. Nelli combined strong piety with a great fondness for classical studies, and also had modest aspirations as a writer and scholar on the Petrarchan model. He was an eager correspondent — we have about fifty of his letters to Petrarch and about thirty-eight of Petrarch's to him.

The close relations of the two men began in 1350 when Petrarch visited Florence on his way back from Rome. But Petrarch would mention some years later (see letter 17) that in fact they had first met in Avignon when Nelli was young and inexperienced — probably in the period 1341-1343. Petrarch unburdened himself to Nelli on the theme of Avignon-Babylon far more than to anyone else. Six of the nineteen letters of the *Liber sine nomine* were addressed to him; and it was to Nelli, apparently, that Petrarch intended to dedicate a special work on the subject of corruption in Avignon, a work that he never wrote. It is in this letter, in fact, that we get our first mention of the idea of such a work; it would be a story, Petrarch says, far more terrible than the tales told by Seneca, and one about which all historians, so often at odds, will agree.

If only my other duties would allow it! At no other time has there ever been a subject so ideal to write about and at the same time to rage over, not to say bewail. What shall I say? It pains me to have started, but it shames me not to go on. And so, though the stars are not propitious, nevertheless now that I have "yoked the oxen," as they say, I shall have to plough over this piece of paper, all too small for my purpose.

"Every vice has reached its peak," writes the Satirist.[1] You simple soul, you certainly had not seen our age! Now, and only now, have the vices reached their peak, beyond which they cannot go without destroying society. You have therefore applied to your own time a complaint more applicable to another. Whatever distress of the historians or lamentation of the tragic dramatists has come to our notice, it was nothing compared with what lies here before our very eyes. A crime which called for high tragedy with them is merely a venial sin with us. God is angry with the world, and the world deserves it; I marvel rather at God's great indulgence. In the old days Fortune toyed with us; now she

[1] JUVENAL, *Sat.* I, 149.

is on the rampage. Send back Nero, I pray, send back Domitian! The persecution will be more open, but it will be lighter and quicker. At least one may then purchase heaven with one's life, a small price to pay, and achieve glory as a martyr. But as it is, we are being destroyed by a spreading plague. We lose not our lives but our virtue. We are allowed neither to live uprightly nor to die honourably. I see it now — Julian[2] has returned from the land of the dead, and he is worse now that he has taken a new name. He holds to the same old viewpoint and hides his evil intent under cover of friendship. Marching behind our banners we are betrayed, and under the guidance of our leader we hasten to our destruction; and if Christ does not come again to redeem us, it is all over with.

Alas, my dearest friend, what do you think, or consider, or discern, or even conjecture must be the state of my mind? It is a miracle that with this poison spread throughout my system I have not turned an unnatural saffron colour, or indeed have not become completely jaundiced. But it is not fear or respect or affection, neither the unspoken threat of punishment for telling the truth nor the promise of reward for lying, that stops me from speaking out about what I know. Rather, it is preoccupation with other business, as well as anger, resentment and distress, the enemies of creativity. Would that my pen were equal to the matter, and that my affairs were sufficiently in order that I might have enough time. Certainly, I would lack neither the vigour nor the passion. I would tell no fables, even though they might seem more like fables than the truth. I would describe monsters which I have seen and heard, which have infected my eyes and ears. I would tell of no one madness, no one raging Hercules, no one Thyes-

---

[2] The emperor Julian the Apostate, A.D.361-363.

tian feast, no one monstrous and loathsome coupling, no one quarrel between greedy brothers, no one hater of the innocent or slayer of wife and mother, the impiety and wantonness of no one parent who deserts her children, no one Troy fallen, no one Hippolytus torn to pieces by the order of an evil father.[3] Rather I would tell of the whole world overturned and mangled. The things that others have to hunt for all over meet you here on every street corner. Do you think I lack a subject for a tragic poem?

Others have commemorated the fortunes of individuals and have written of particular crimes; but what I have to celebrate in verse — or better, lament — are the unheard-of tales without number, the misfortune, enslavement, fall, mockery and death of all human kind. The truest history will emerge, but it will be tragic and frightful. The Linen Books[4] will agree with the annals; there will be no conflict among Polybius and Claudius and Licinius and Valerius Antias, nor between Sallust and Livy, Herodotus and Thucydides, but "all are in accord," to use Aristotle's words. I shall write, Truth will dictate, all mankind will be witness. You, Posterity, you be the judge, unless, as it happens, you are so overwhelmed by the evils of your own day that you cannot be bothered with ours.

Meanwhile my friend, if I know you at all, from this brief outline you will have a clear idea not only of everything I write but of everything I think. You need no other work of tragedy or history. Keep well, and consider yourself lucky that you are not here!

---

[3] This is a brief summary of the subjects of most of Seneca's Tragedies: *Hercules Furens, Thyestes, Oedipus, Phoenissae, Octavia, Medea, Troades* and *Hippolytus*.
[4] An ancient chronicle of the Roman people written on linen, to which Livy frequently referred.

7

It used to be thought that this letter was written to Cola di Rienzo, but its place in the collection and the whole tone of the letter make such an identification very uncertain. That the recipient is an Italian is probable, but it seems likely that he is a high-ranking ecclesiastic. A good case has been made for thinking that it was Niccola di Capocci, cardinal-priest of St. Vitalis.[1]

The bright and glorious venture that Petrarch mentions here, and which he hopes to share in, may well have been connected with the preparation of a brief on the condition of Rome which we know he was asked to draw up for a special commission of four cardinals. One of the four, the only one who was an Italian, was Niccola di Capocci.

When I think back on that most pious and profound talk we had the day before yesterday, just outside the gates of that ancient temple of religion, I glow with eagerness and fall into such a state that I imagine I heard the oracle of some divinity whose advice had been sought, its voice issuing forth from the depths of a temple. I seem to have heard a god, not a man. I heard you lament, as though inspired, the present condition, indeed the collapse and ruin, of the state, while you so profoundly and eloquently probed our wounds. Ever since then, every time I recall the sound of your voice my soul grows heavy, my eyes become moist; and my heart, which burned while then you spoke, now dissolves into tears when I think back and reflect on what you said, and then ponder the future — not womanly tears, but strong, virile tears which will venture some act of honour if the chance arise, and leap forth in manly fashion in the defence of justice.

[1] See E.H. WILKINS, *Studies,* pp. 186-192.

As often, therefore, as I may have been in the past, I am now more than ever with you in spirit, especially since that day. Often despair comes over me, often hope; often my spirit wavers between the two, and I cry: Oh, if ever... oh, if it might only happen in my lifetime! Oh, if I could take part in such a bright and glorious venture!

Then turning again and again to the crucified one who is my delight, with mournful voice and tearful eyes I cry out: Oh good Jesus, you are too indulgent. What can this be? "Arise! why do you sleep? Arise! Do not cast us off forever! Why do you hide your face? Why do you forget our affliction and our oppression?" (Ps. 43, 23). Oh God our protector, look down upon us. See what we suffer, and whence it comes, and what your enemies do under cover of your name. Look down, and take your revenge. If not, then help us before the force of the death-dealing poison has robbed our limbs of life and we are overcome by the infinite weight of evils. What are you doing, oh Salvation of those who hope in you? (Ps. 16, 7). What, oh Saviour, do you ponder; what do you hesitate over? How long will you turn your eyes from us? How long will you remain unmoved by our wretchedness? How long before you put an end to such great suffering? Do you not see the evils which have befallen us, you from whom nothing is hidden beneath the arch of heaven or in the depths of the abyss — not the drops of the ocean, the leaves of the forest, not each grain of sand, the stars above, the plants beneath, the whole multitude of living things? Do you now hate us, you who used to love us, you who were so overcome by love of us that from heaven where you reigned as God you came down to earth as man in order to die on the cross? Or does it happen that you do see these things, and do love us still, but lack the strength to help us? But if you are not omni-

potent, then what hope do we have? Or do you fear the strength
of your enemies? But surely, the arrogance of our world has not
raised men to be the equals of God! Or do you withhold
your judgement out of mercy? Then take care, infallible judge,
that in sparing the few you do not destroy an infinite number,
and that while you are compassionate to the wicked you are
not cruel to the good and bring disaster to the innocent.

But what am I saying, a mere man? Who am I to quarrel
with you? To you we entrust ourselves and all we own.
You who created us will look after us, mindful that our
feebleness cannot stand up long under the burden of such
great tribulations. Therefore bring us help while there is time,
while there still remains anyone to benefit from it, so that you
may not have to restore those whom you could have kept safe,
as you will have to do if you let them perish. Come, our one
hope, and as we say in our daily prayer, "make haste to help us."[1]
Destroy the world's many evils, we pray, or else destroy the
world itself.

8

Petrarch wrote this letter to Ildebrandino, bishop of Padua,
with whom he had become very close after receiving a canonry in
the church of Padua in 1349. Ildebrandino was a member of the
noble Roman family of Conti. He became bishop of Padua in
1319, although he left the administration of the diocese to a
vicar until 1332 while he remained in Avignon where he was
probably employed in the curia. Again in 1342 he was to be found
in the service of the Avignonese court, returning to his see only in
1347. He died in Padua on November 2, 1352.

---

[2] The opening prayer of each hour of the divine office, from Ps. 69, 2.

The themes of Babylon and the labyrinth to be found here will be much further developed elsewhere, especially in letter 10. Here, however, we have a reflection of a conversation that Petrarch had had with the bishop early in 1351. Ildebrandino urged Petrarch not to go to Avignon, to ignore the call that he had received from two cardinals (it was in another letter that Petrarch mentions them as "two powerful bulls lording it over Christ's wide pastures"), to abandon worldly ambition and avoid the rat-race of curial responsibility of which the bishop himself had had ample experience — all in vain. Whatever it was that the bishop warned against, Petrarch was willing to undertake. Apparently, too, he felt that he could be of some benefit to his friends by going to Avignon.

Whatever he wanted, however, he soon ceased to want. As mentioned above in the Introduction, there is good reason to believe that it was a cardinal's hat. What he actually got was an offer of a job as apostolic secretary. Something of his embarrassment can be discerned in the last few lines of the letter.

If I should want to put into writing everything I feel about the state of this western Babylon whose inhabitant I have so often become quite against my will — through fate, or more truly for my sins — I fear, father, that I would increase my grief by my lamentations and disturb your most holy cares and sacred duties with untimely and pointless complaints. In all, you may be sure that the task is too great not only for my pen, but even for that of a Cicero. Whatever you may have read of the Babylons of Assyria or Egypt, of the four labyrinths, of the portals of Avernus and the forests and sulphurous marshes of the lower world, is all child's play compared with this hell. Here you may see Nimrod, a turret-rearing terror;[1] Semiramis armed with her quiver;[2] merciless Minos, Rhadaman-

---

[1] A reference to pope Clement VI, who built a large addition to the papal palace of his predecessor.

[2] *Pharetrata Semiramis.* The expression may be found in Juvenal, *Sat.* II, 108, where the context has to do with effeminacy and homosexuality.

thus, and all-consuming Cerberus; "here is Pasiphaë coupled with the bull," to quote Vergil, "and the mongrel offspring and two-formed progeny, the Minotaur, memorial of her foul love."[3] Finally you may see here every disorder, gloom, or horror to be found or imagined anywhere. You have always been fortunate in your virtues; oh, how much more fortunate you are in not being here! Do you think this is the same city you used to know? Far from it; it is quite different! At that time it was certainly the worst and foulest of cities; now, it is not so much a city as a dwelling place of shadows and spectres — in a word, the sink of every crime and scandal, that "living hell" which David prophesied in his psalm long before it was founded or known (Ps. 54, 15).

Ah, how often have I recalled your fatherly voice and your wise warning when you said to me as I was preparing to depart: "Where are you going? What are you striving for? What ambition drives you on, unmindful of your own good? Don't you know what you're getting into and what you're leaving behind? Will you knowingly go off to a task unworthy of you? Look closely, I beg of you, at what you're doing, where you're rushing. If I know you at all, you'll be sorry for your haste. You know full well the snares of the court; once you get caught, you won't be able to get out when you wish."

And what did I reply to these and like arguments of yours? Nothing other than that I was returning to well-known afflictions, compelled by the love of friends. That is what I said. I did not lie, and I do not now repent of that love. But I am not sure whether I regret that I ranked my freedom lower than the convenience of my friends. At all events, I owe you heartfelt thanks for your advice, hitherto so poorly

---

[3] *Aeneid*, VI, 24-6.

heeded and lately proved so sound. I have been punished for not obeying it at the time. But I shall be more obedient in future, if ever I get away from here. I have not given up hope of succeeding, if Christ stretches forth his right hand, and to this I am bending every effort.

Shame prevented me, father, from writing these things to you earlier. For it is shameful and unbecoming in a man to want what he soon after does not want.

9

The following two letters were both sent to Francesco Nelli in Florence, this one in November-December, 1351, and the next one on or shortly after January 13, 1352. They are quite different in character, letter 9 breathing a kind of apocalyptic vengeance, letter 10 more coolly pursuing the twin intellectual conceits of Babylon III and Labyrinth V.

Despite the attraction that Petrarch's ideas of Italian unity held for nineteenth-century nationalists, his political notions here as elsewhere are vague and undeveloped. Apparently either God or Fortune would invest all Italians with a common will, whereupon the past glories of the Roman empire would somehow be revived.

It is the *super flumina Babylonis*, "by the rivers of Babylon," at the end of letter 9 that Nelli must have puzzled over, to judge from the opening, and indeed the entire theme, of letter 10.

Afflictions are of two kinds: those we suffer unwillingly, and those we accept willingly. Perhaps some one else would claim that there are more than two, and certainly there are an infinite number of afflictions as anyone who has lived for any length of time knows. All of them, however, come down to these two: the voluntary and the imposed. Unwillingly we suffer exile, poverty, theft, sickness, imprisonment, servitude, disgrace, chains, torture, the axe, the sword, death. Willingly we submit ourselves to the yoke of vice and often put ourselves at the beck and call of the vilest men either from craven fear, shameful sloth, disgraceful indifference, or disgusting hope of profit. From the examples I have given you see what I mean, and you can add to the list. To many, the first type, the unwilling kind, seems the worse, but to me the second is the worse, where, that is, it is a question of an offence and the calamity therefore occasions no pity.

It is precisely by this latter burden of affliction that a groaning Italy is now enslaved. She will finally put an end to her wretchedness only when she begins to will herself to be united. A difficult condition, certainly, but by no means impossible. For when I say "united," I do not mean that this will be achieved simply by aspiring to unity but by putting her aspirations into effect and ending her unworthy servitude. Ye Gods, we used to rule the greatest peoples! Look how we have fallen! Now we are the slaves of the worst! What a hard fate! What an unbearable change! But you barbarians[1] — forever foolish, now crazed madmen — you scoff at your queen, Italy. If only the same spirit moved everyone as it does me, with greater wisdom but no less passion, then indeed we should quickly sweep aside trivialities and get down to serious business. Almighty God will see to it, if he does not yet detest us to a man. Fortune will see to it if there be any such thing as Fortune, and if indeed she has any control over human events. If, however, you ask me to dig up a deeper truth and tell you what I think: they mock with their lips but groan in their hearts; they joke on the surface, but tremble inside, for they know both us and themselves, and feign contempt to hide their hatred and fear.

---

[1] The French in the curia in Avignon.

Where do my words lead, you may ask? I write, not because you have to hear about it, but because I cannot remain silent. It is a great and grievous burden and I can deposit it in no other ear with more confidence than in yours. I, an angry exile from Jerusalem,[2] living by the rivers of Babylon, have written these things to you in great haste.

10

You are surprised by the addresses on my letters. As well you might be. Since you have read of only two Babylons, the Assyrian one of long ago enshrining the famous name of Semiramis, and the Egyptian one founded by Cambyses which still flourishes in our own day, you wonder about this unheard-of Babylon with which you are now confronted. You know that some of our authors declared Rome to be another Babylon, so to speak, on account of a similarity of government and climate; but since, as you say, I usually refer to Rome as our holy mother, queen of cities, you are now puzzled by this newest of Babylons.

You can stop wondering. This part of the world has its own Babylon. For where, I ask, may the "city of confusion" (Gen. 11, 9) be more appropriately located than in the west? We do not know who founded it, but it is well known who inhabits it — those, surely, from whom for the best of reasons it derives this name. Believe me, this place has its Nimrod too, "powerful in the land and robust hunter against the Lord" (Gen. 10, 8-12), reaching heavenward with his proud

2 From Rome and Italy.

turrets; here is Semiramis armed with her quiver; here is a
Cambyses madder than the eastern one who first drove his
chariot over the necks of kings but later, worn out from
feasting and surfeited by the slaughter of his men, was reduced
from haughty lordship to wretched poverty.[1] I shall not refer
you to the poets — no need of the Muses here — nor to the
historians. Look to catholic authors, especially to Augustine's
commentary on that psalm which begins in the same way[2] I
end some of my letters to you. There you will find out what
the name Babylon meant to him. After you read it you will
agree that the name fits the Rhone as well as it does the
Euphrates or the Nile. Nor will you continue to marvel if
you remember how Ambrose used the name when he spoke
of the Rhone in that work of his where he mourns the
untimely death of the younger Valentinian.[3]

Now that I have uprooted this amazement of yours, let me
shake up another one: you can indeed be surprised by five
labyrinths when other authors, I believe, mention only four.
They know of those in Egypt, Lemnos, Crete and Clusium in
Italy, but they say nothing of the labyrinth of the Rhone,
the most confusing and by far the worst of all,
either because it did not yet exist, or because it was not yet
known. I constantly refer to it — how justly, anyone who
wishes to know may learn by coming here. Here is the dreadful
prison, the aimless wandering in the dwelling place of shadows,
the urn in which Fate stirs the lots of men, tyrannical Minos,
and the voracious Minotaur, memorial of forbidden love —

---

[1] Among those who sought the mysterious source of the Nile was the mad
Cambyses who got as far as Ethiopia when his food ran out and he was forced
to feed on his own men. See LUCAN, *De bello civili*, X, 279-283.

[2] *Super flumina Babylonis* (Ps. 136).

[3] *De obitu Valentiniani consolatio*, 79, in MIGNE, *Patrologia Latina*, XVI, 1443.

but no healing medicine, no love, no charity, no promises worthy of trust, no friendly counsel, no thread as a silent guide to mark the twisted path, no Ariadne, no Daedalus. There is only one hope of salvation here, gold. Gold placates the savage king and overcomes the frightful monster; the guiding cord is woven of gold; gold reveals the forbidding doorway, shatters the bars and stones, bribes the stern doorkeeper, and opens the gates of heaven. What else? Christ is sold for gold.

11

This letter was written to Rinaldo Cavalchini of Villafranca (c. 1290 - c. 1362), one of a small circle of humanists and poets at the court of the della Scala in Verona. He had once been tutor to Petrarch's son Giovanni.

The letter was written late in 1351 or early in 1352, obviously in reply to an enquiry from Rinaldo who seems to have desired some appointment in or by the papal curia and to have been prepared to come to Avignon. Petrarch's response is predictable: your poverty, he says, is enviable compared with the rotten riches of Avignon. He would, however, do his best for his friend provided Rinaldo got his petition to him as quickly as possible, for he had no intention of staying in Avignon any longer than he had to.

I do not know where to begin, or indeed whether to begin; and I often think of that line: "should I speak or remain silent?"[1] Well, I shall speak; then you will not conclude from my silence either that you are being neglected out of laziness or held in low esteem out of insolence. But where to start? and on what to dwell? Or rather, what *not* to speak about? So many currents pull me this way and that, warring against one

[1] *Aeneid*, III, 39.

another and making it difficult to choose. I have no time to respond to all the pressures, for they are infinite. And even if I did have, it would be dangerous to do so. And so, though I may not be held back by my duties and cares which, as you know, are many and demanding, fear alone is enough to excuse my pen.

Where virtue does not reign, truth has always remained weak, naked and helpless. What happens, do you think, where virtue has been completely·destroyed and long since buried? Truth actually becomes the greatest of crimes. Nothing more is needed to earn the hatred of many people, though to win the affection of just one person takes all kinds of solicitation. You have to be deferential to many if you want many to like you; but to be hated by many takes little effort. You do not have to take up weapons, or lunge at the enemy; an unbridled tongue is weapon enough, and to speak the truth is to inflict a wound. Why not, where there is no one to whom a true word can be spoken without arousing a violent reproach; where no piety dwells, no charity, no faith; where passion reigns and malice, vice and greed, with all the manner of life that goes with them; where whoever is the worst is promoted, the open-handed thief is praised to heaven, the honest pauper is oppressed; where frankness is called foolishness, cunning is called wisdom, God is despised, money worshipped, the laws trodden underfoot, and good men so ridiculed that it now appears that there is almost no good man left to be ridiculed.

What an immoral age! What a sad and wretched place of exile this is! What happy eyes you have, not to have to look at such things! Yours is a most joyful labour compared with this disgusting and rotten leisure; yours is a most enviable poverty compared with these riches, evilly gathered and evilly spent. There is an old saying about the coin falling into the

sewer.[2] If anyone does not understand it, let him come here
where he may read it along with a thousand others equally
famous written on everyone's face. There is one person here
whom I would gladly exempt from this universal flood of
crimes, and quite deservedly so; but it is obviously foolish
to modify such a well-established and general pattern simply
because there is some one person to whom it does not apply.[3]
So no Noah, no Deucalion, will swim to safety; and in case you
think that Pyrrha had any better luck on the water, you
can be sure that no one is going to stay afloat. A torrent
of the most obscene passions, an unbelievable storm of lewdness, and the foulest shipwreck of chastity without exception
has enveloped them all alike.

Truth, having overcome fear, has ventured these few complaints out of many; from these you may deduce others still
hidden under a veil of silence. If, however, you have any
confidence that by the aid of a friend anything to your benefit
can be gotten out of this place, as medicine from certain
noxious animals or plants, write instantly. Do not delay. For
I am hurrying as fast as I can to reach the door of this
hopeless labyrinth. Already, if I am not mistaken, I have in my
hands the one thing that anyone can hope to find here, the
thread of a noble contempt.[4] If I know what you want,

[2] "Money falls into the hands of some men like a coin falling into a sewer."
SENECA, *Ad Lucilium epistulae morales,* LXXXVII, 16.

[3] Elsewhere Petrarch remarks: "it is my view ... that the force of a general truth
is not destroyed by a very few exceptional instances" (*De vita solitaria,* I, iii, 2,
in Jacob ZEITLIN [tr.], *The Life of Solitude* [Urbana: University of Illinois Press,
1924], p. 126).

[4] Referring to the thread that guided Daedalus out of the labyrinth. What
Petrarch seems to mean is that his contempt for Avignon is in itself a guarantee
of eventual escape. He had a longer stay ahead of him than he here seems
to think he has, for he did not finally get away until May, 1353.

I shall strain every nerve to attain it in the time left. But in such darkness as this I see no benefit to you or to me other than in flight.

Your pupil[5] wishes to greet you. Would that he were with you, though perhaps it is better to have him here with me, so that right from his tender years he might learn to abhor this abominable pit, this truly hellish prison. Thus he will never be taken unawares, as I was when I was so young — I know not whether for my sins or my parents', though if mine I was still too young to have committed them. I have often escaped, only to fall back into bondage over and over again. Now at last I am captive by my own will — no longer a child, indeed an old man — and have no one to blame but myself.

To this letter, however, I have put neither my hand, nor my seal, nor the place of writing, nor the date. You know where I am. You recognize my voice.

12

This letter was written to Philippe de Cabassoles, the recipient of letter 1. It is an anguished psalmodic utterance, bewailing the fate of Christ's people (by whom Petrarch seems to mean not all Christians but rather Italians) who for one moment had been freed by the death of Pope Clement VI only to be plunged into servitude again by the election of Pope Innocent VI. We hoped, he says, that with the death of the pope God would humble the proud and cast out the wolves from among the sheep, but instead God's enemies remain in proud possession of their power, i.e. the French in the curia are still lording it over us. The letter was obviously written very shortly after Innocent's election, which took place on December 8, 1352.

---

[5] Petrarch's son, Giovanni.

By this time Petrarch had already decided to leave Provence. Only a month earlier he had actually set out for Italy, but was forced to turn back because of a wild storm and news of bandits on the route. Among much else that he detested in Avignon and drove him to consider leaving had been the slanderous accusation that he was a necromancer.[1] Innocent VI had been one of those who believed the charge. On more than one occasion after Petrarch finally left Avignon his friends in the curia tried to coax Innocent into abandoning his unwarranted distrust of the poet and to offer him a curial post. It took them some nine years before they were successful. "Who would not be amazed," Petrarch would write to one of the cardinals who had consistently supported him,

> and at the same time overjoyed, to become a friend of that vicar of Christ who not only is wont to suspect but openly to maintain that I am a necromancer; and to learn that this opinion of me, falsely conceived and hitherto stubbornly held against your eloquent pleading and that of many another who wished to root it out, has now suddenly not simply been abandoned, but completely reversed, so that he now seeks by gifts and entreaties private intercourse with, and the faithful service of, one whose every word and every sight he once loathed?

A malicious cardinal had spread the rumour, he went on. "He said that I was skilled in magic, and did not blush to offer as proof that I read, or had read, Vergil; and the pope believed it. To think, that the greatest affairs have been entrusted to such mentalities!" Petrarch recalled to his friend how they used to joke about it, in the very presence of Innocent before he had been elected pope. Later, after Innocent's election, when Petrarch was about to leave Provence and went in to Avignon to say good-bye to his friends, he refused to pay a call on the pope as he was urged to do,

---

[1] For references to Petrarch's letter in which the charge of necromancy is mentioned, see E.H. WILKINS, *Studies*, pp. 145-146.

fearing, he said, that "my magic might have annoyed him, his credulity me."[2]

Petrarch had much to be unhappy about, therefore, with Innocent's election. This entire letter is a measure of his crushing disappointment.

Woe to your people, oh Christ Jesus, woe to your people, oh Christ! Oh fount of mercies, let us come before you to bewail our misfortunes. In the way of wounded lovers, the more desperately we love the more hopefully we complain. If it is proper for half-dead worms to complain about the Lord of hosts, graciously accept our prayers and have mercy upon us, you who alone can. We complain not as your accusers but as your humble petitioners, in tearful prostration before your eternal throne. Still we complain, and we pray that you will listen to our lamentations without offense and in your loving kindness give heed to your petitioners.

There is no need for lengthy words, or indeed for any words at all. You know our thoughts not only before we utter them but even before we think them. Not only do you see the condition of your people, you who see all things; but what we find even more grievous and shameful, so do our enemies. And in their insolence they say: "'God has left them; pursue and seize them, for there is no one to deliver them.' Oh God, do not withdraw from us; our God, look to our aid" (Ps. 70, 11-12), not merely to observe us, but to have pity on us and bring us help. Look upon our distress; we are in the last throes, because in your indescribable mercy you placed your trust in us, with the result that we fragile earthen vessels have turned against you, the immortal potter (Isaiah, 29, 16).

---

[2] Norman P. ZACOUR, *Talleyrand: The Cardinal of Périgord (1301-1364)* (Transactions of the American Philosophical Society, L, part 7, 1960), pp.29-30.

Surely, if you who created us to hold a place of honour now bring us into contempt, it will be a much sharper punishment than is your custom, even though we deserve it. If you let others humble us so, you have become much more tolerant of our sufferings than usual. If you ignore us, you have become neglectful of your people far beyond the usual. And if you have come to hate us, what then has happened to that love of yours which brought you to die for us so gladly? But if, perhaps, you toy with us, make sure that your game is not rougher than is reasonable; take care that we are not too weak to stand the strain. For you are the conquering "lion of the tribe of Judah" (Apoc. 5, 5), while we are the "sheep of your pasture" (Ps. 73, 1). You can see how unfair the contest is. If you do not stop acting the lion you will exhaust us with your playfulness and destroy us.

If, however, you are angry with us, we do not deny that we deserve it. But what of those words about you in which we have trusted, given to us out of the mouth of your prophet: "When you are angry, remember your mercy" (Habakkuk, 3, 2)? Remember, oh Lord, remember your mercy and overlook our sins! Such befits you; such will help us. We deserve, I confess, every punishment — in fact, no punishment is great enough for our sins. We have done those things for which you punish us deservedly and justly; and we know that while you are extremely just you are also twice as merciful. This is why, with good reason, before calling you "just" your prophet said that you were merciful and compassionate. "There is arisen," he says, "a light in the darkness for the upright, gracious and compassionate," — and then adds, "and just" (Ps. 111, 4). When he said elsewhere: "Gracious is the Lord, and just," seeing these two attributes side by side he immediately added: "and our God is merciful." (Ps. 114, 5).

He put anger in the middle, and set up twin barriers of mercy on each side and walled around the anger so that it could not operate unchecked by mercy. Therefore, merciful Jesus Christ, do not reverse them, we beseech you; do not loose your unchecked anger, the force of which you have enclosed within your mercy, upon your servants, even though they be stubborn. Do not lock up your mercy within your anger, but unmindful of our offenses have mercy upon us. "Have you cast us off forever, oh Lord? Are you cutting us off from your compassion forevermore, from generation unto generation? Have you forgotten how to be merciful, oh God, or will you shut up your mercies in your anger?" (Ps. 76, 8-10). But see, oh Lord, the prophet's cry is not that you shut up your mercies in your anger, but rather the reverse; he has chosen his words with care, not by chance. Hence what I have been saying: the anger is one, the mercies many.

Therefore, "magnify your merits unto us, you who save those who trust in you. Save us as the pupil of your eye — save us with your right hand from those who rise up against you" (Ps. 16, 7-8). You were compassionate to the Jewish people, who have always been ungrateful to you, by parting the Red Sea and leading them home. Part our Red Sea also, and in the sight of all those who have held us captive bestow your mercies upon us, your new chosen people, who, as ungrateful as we may also be, yet glory in your name. Save us, oh Lord, that we may know at first hand the mercies of the Lord, "and praise you for your mercies" (Ps. 106, 15). "Let your mercy reach us soon, for we are brought very low. Help us, oh God of our salvation," not for our merits but "for the glory of your name. Deliver us and be forgiving of our sins," not because we are worthy, but "for your name's sake, and that it may not be said among the heathen," as it is now: "'Where is their God?'" (Ps. 78, 8-10). For where are your mercies of old, the mercies of the Lord, which we shall praise forever, in which we have always trusted, in which we still have hope?

But what is this, oh Lord, that you do now? "You shattered the brass gates of our captivity and broke asunder the bars of iron" (Ps. 106, 16), and by your decree from on high, oh king eternal, you freed our shackled feet bound in poverty and iron.[3] Why do you allow new chains to be forged for us from the same metal?[4] "You destroyed the old net" (Ps. 123, 7); why have you allowed another to be woven from the same hemp? You lifted from us a heavy, evil and repulsive yoke; why do you place on us yet another unbearable yoke carved from the same tree? "You have laid affliction on our backs, and men over our heads" (Ps. 65, 11-12) — oh, if only they were men and not starved and savage animals! In tears we pray, "do not deliver up the souls of those who confess your name to the beasts; do not forget forever the souls of the congregation of your poor" (Ps. 73, 19). "You have cast us out and destroyed us. You are angry. Have mercy upon us. You have made the earth tremble and have thrown it into confusion. Heal its griefs, for it has been badly shaken indeed. You have shown your people hard things" (Ps. 59, 3-5). "You have tried us in fire as silver is tried. We went through fire and water. Bring us to our refuge" (Ps. 65, 10, 12). Do not deprive us of our most just expectation. For we trusted in you that you would calm the lashing of the seas (in which fortunately that old fisherman finally perished) once his vessel had passed to his successor, for you control the force of the sea; and we trusted that

---

[3] By decreeing the death of Clement VI.
[4] By allowing the election of Innocent VI.

you would "humble the proud and overthrow your enemies with your strong arm" (Ps. 88, 11), cast out the wolves from among the sheep, the pirates from among the fishermen, the thieves from among the faithful shepherds. But instead, the pride of them that hate you grows always! Thus far, my words have been addressed to God.

But you, father,[5] who especially share my grief, do not give in to Fortune, but until she has given her changeable wheel a better turn — which we recently hoped she would do — try to carry on and remain firm, so that when our time comes to leave this world we may carry a happier tale to the souls of the blessed.

13

To judge from the opening, this may be only part of a longer letter that has since disappeared. There are hardly any clues to the identity of its recipient, other than the twice-used expression "as you see" *(ut vides)*, which suggests that he may have been in or near Avignon, and the reference to "our" Syracuse, which indicates some connection with the kingdom of Naples (Sicily). He shared Petrarch's interest in the classics sufficiently to catch the allusion to Juvenal, and he shared, too, in a kind of private code when alluding to public figures in Avignon — Dionysius, Semiramis, Pericles, Alcibiades — the identities of whom remain difficult to establish with certainty.[1]

As you see, things go on — or rather, they don't go on, they're dragged on. Virtue is no protection, justice has perished,

5 Now addressing Philippe de Cabassoles.
1 See John E. WRIGLEY, "A Rehabilitation of Clement VI: Sine Nomine 13 and the Kingdom of Naples," *Archivum historiae pontificiae,* III (1965), 127-138.

freedom is dead, fairness is vanquished; lust reigns, greed rages, envy boils. Every class of men is afflicted with its own tyrants. Though born to sing the praises of God with our lips and in our hearts, we live out our whole lives in jealous strife. Because of our sins that glorious temple of Jesus Christ, once an impregnable fortress of the divine cult, has now become at last a den of savage thieves, destitute of heavenly aid. Yes, the origin of the evil flows from a single source; it is joined by other lesser streams, from all of which there boils up a huge torrent of every kind of misery. We must soon perish, overcome in a vast flood of evils, and if divine love does not bring an end to the faithlessness of mankind, the church will suffer a tragic shipwreck. How different in manner are those who build from those who destroy — what a contrast in outlook! May almighty God provide for his dwelling-place, for I have nothing to oppose to the very many who strive against it except the compassion one owes to a mother, and an escape which, as you see, is a relief to me, freeing my eyes from such a sorrowful sight. I see from a distance the cruel and notorious craft by which that ecclesiastical Dionysius torments and despoils our Syracuse; but being unable to prevent it, I refuse to look at it close at hand. I see how this imitation Semiramis covers her head with a man's crown, and with what artifice she dazzles the eyes of all bystanders; and how, defiled by incestuous embraces, she tramples men underfoot.[2] I see with what arts this Pericles of ours protects

---

[2] Elsewhere, Petrarch is a little more specific about the shameful behaviour of the original Semiramis, who murdered her husband and later sought the embraces of her own son who killed her in his outraged shame. See the brief biography he wrote of her, published by Pierre DE NOLHAC, "Le *De viris illustribus* de Pétrarque," *Notices et extraits de manuscrits de la Bibliothèque nationale*, XXXIV, i (Paris, 1895), 119-121; there is also a brief reference to her in *Fam.* IV, 4, Rossi II, 218.

himself, so that he need not render an account for what cannot be accounted for. He has his Alcibiades, quicker than any to support his evil designs. He deliberately upsets and confuses everything; for what other reason, do you think, than that he may the more freely practice his deceptions like a side-show barker distracting attention with his whip or raising a cloud of dust, hiding his crime under the cover of the state's confusion? Certainly, because of the nature of his schemes, he uses no new arts, for the birdcatcher thrives in shrubbery, the fisherman in troubled waters, the thief in darkness. What more wretched future could I wish for us in our lethargy than that we remain just as we are with only our noses awake, snoring in our cups before the adulterer![3] I confess that I do not know which is more shameful, his impudence or our indulgence.

14

Petrarch had left Avignon and was living in Milan when he wrote this letter sometime between 1353 and 1356. We do not know to whom it was addressed. Whoever it was had apparently visited Avignon after Petrarch's departure. His visit gave Petrarch an opportunity to expatiate on the evils of Avignon, that living hell, calling on his correspondent as witness to the truth of his observations, and including a remarkable anecdote about two cardinals surrounded by a crowd of office-seekers which must have been a common sight outside the papal palace.

The recipient of letter 14 was obviously a bishop whose visit to Avignon, since he had never been there before, may have been occasioned by his recent election. He was apparently a native of Padua who had studied law at Bologna in his youth. But

---

[3] Referring to the compliant husband in JUVENAL, *Sat.* I, 55 ff., who was trained to ignore his wife's well-paid services to other men.

whatever diocese was now in his charge seems not to have been in Italy. "Ad nos veni," Petrarch writes — "come to us" — by which he could not have meant Milan in particular (where he himself was), for he elaborated the invitation with a list of specific places, all of them Italian cities, which included Milan. He seems, therefore, to have meant Italy in general.

I put off writing you for a long time, looking for both a topic and a courier. Although it is unusual for one or the other not to be at hand (seeing that you are generosity itself and that I, for all my lack of talent, am no miser when it comes to writing), still on this occasion I lacked them both at one and the same time. But now the courier is here, and a better one you won't find anywhere. No one is more devoted to you, or more familiar to me. Now I have a subject to write about: the news of your long, difficult and disagreeable trip, which might have prompted my pen long before this except that I had no idea where in the world you were to be found. For I was neither persuaded that you would want to stay long in that land of the dead, nor was I at all able to believe that you had gone there unless forced by the demand of some pressing need. So in silence I excused a journey required by her[1] who often burdens the necks of kings and popes with a yoke as hard as steel. Now that I can rejoice at your safe return, my confidence in that friendship which your esteem has held out to me allows me to ask what the best of men has to do with the worst of places: what have you to do with Babylon? We read that the bravest Romans usually avoided Baiae in Campania even though it was warm and healthful, because it was as

---

[1] Necessity. See HORACE, *Carm.* III, 24, 5-8

empty of decency as it was full of pleasures and delights to
say the least; and so, forgetful of everything else, they
concentrated upon a single-minded pursuit of virtue. This
being the case, who shouldn't avoid the Rhone? Who, I ask,
shouldn't flee Babylon, sorrowful dwelling of all vice, distress
and utter wretchedness? I certainly ought to know something about it!

I speak of things I have seen, not just heard about. As
a boy it was my evil fate to be carried off to that country
where, despite my revulsion, I was bound until recently
by what shackles of Fortune I do not know. There I passed
many years in sorrow. I know from experience that there
is no piety there, no charity, no faith, no reverence or fear
of God, nothing sacred, nothing just, nothing reasonable,
nothing serious — in a word, nothing human. Love, modesty,
decency, honesty are banished from the place. As for truth,
I remain silent; for what room is there for truth, where
everything is full of lies: air, land, houses, towers, streets,
courtyards, squares, porches, vestibules, halls, rooms, the
ceilings, the cracks in the walls, the public lodginghouses,
the church sanctuaries, the courts of justice, the seats of
pontiffs — even men's mouths, their nods, gestures, voices,
their faces, their very souls. Now what do you say? Am
I lying, or am I telling the truth about lying? If, being there
and undistracted by your important affairs, you looked closely
and critically on that abominable parade of wickedness, I shall
need no other judge as to how everything there is bereft of
virtue and truth and is full of crime, intrigue, deceit, flattery
and the evillest wiles of ambition and avarice, of pride and
malice. You saw how they carry on all their idle pretences,
not only before men but before God. You marked their sly
smiles masking mournful hearts, their serene brows covering

clouded minds, their soft hands making sharp gestures, their
angelic voices disguising devilish purposes, their sweet songs
uttering from hardened hearts, their honeyed words issuing
from bitter lungs and a dry mouth, scarcely squeezing past
their lips. In all of this there is clearly fulfilled the words of
David: "For their words are softer than oil, yet are darts"
(Ps. 54, 2). Among them not only does lying now go unpunished, but it is a mark of distinction indeed, just as the
cleverer one is in deceit the higher he ranks, and no one dares
rebuke him. I do not wish to pursue this theme in any greater
detail, in case the subject leads my pen to write more than it
should. Besides, the matter is known at large and needs neither
proof nor discussion. I shall confine myself here to one brief
story, enough to the point to illustrate everything else. I myself
was present.

Two of the conscript fathers,[2] on whom the earth's sphere
and the gate of the house of God pivot as on a hinge, came
down together from the papal palace surrounded by a dense
army of servants. A huge crowd of expectant supplicants,
of whom that wretched and God-forsaken city is fuller than
any other, were as usual besieging the stern, unheeding doorway. At the sight of their leaders, in whom they had hope,
they began to raise a cry, each anxiously demanding for
himself what his chances were, or how his request had made
out with the pope. Thereupon one of the cardinals, a notorious fabricator of falsehoods, began to make up all kinds
of things. He was not at all disturbed by the sudden onslaught
(as though accustomed to such things for a long time),[3]

---

[2] Cardinals, likened to the senators of ancient Rome, a common metaphor.
[3] He has obviously been made a cardinal only recently. The chances are that
the incident occurred during Petrarch's last stay in Provence, 1351-1353, and

and was untouched either by any sense of shame or by
commiseration for those wretched people who threw away
their energies, lives, fortune and all their time in such idle
hopes. He pretended that to each there was a remnant of hope
and invented papal responses to the supplications of this
person or that, pursuing each tale with unrelieved impudence
and without the slightest hesitation. They all believed what
they heard and went their way, some delighted, others downcast as the case might be. But the other cardinal, of a nobler
and less shameless nature (one who might have been a good
man if he were not a member of the college), jokingly said
to his colleague: "Aren't you ashamed to delude these simple
men and on your own to make up decisions of the pope, when
you know that we haven't been able to see him either today
or for many days past?" To this that venerable father, the
sly old fox, laughingly replied with the unblushing expression
of a harlot: "Rather, you should be ashamed to be so slow-
witted that you haven't been able in all this time[4] to learn
the arts of the court." At these words I was stupefied, but all
the others were dissolved in laughter, and praising the reply
of that scoundrel they proclaimed him the brightest of men
for having learned so quickly how to lie and cheat.

that he is referring to one of the twelve cardinals appointed in 1350. Given
his outspoken *Invective* written probably in 1355) against Jean de Caraman,
created cardinal deacon of St. George *ad Velum aureum* by Clement VI in 1350,
it is tempting to think that Petrarch is here referring to the same person.
Jean de Caraman was a great-nephew of John XXII; also, one of his cousins
married a nephew of Clement VI in 1350 (E. BALUZE, *Vitae paparum
Avenionensium,* ed. G. Mollat, II [Paris, 1927], 420). At the time of his appointment as a cardinal he had been serving as a papal notary (*ibid.,* I, 256). He
died on August 1, 1361.

[4] Obviously a cardinal of much longer standing than the other.

But I have now ventured into a field far too vast. It calls for a book, not a letter.[5] So I shall drop the subject. Instead, let me now turn my pen to you, good father, and pray, beseech, entreat and adjure you, if you have any esteem for yourself, or thought for your soul, that you never again think of returning there whence no one has ever departed made better by its example, though people without number have come away made much worse. Moreover, if anyone ever came away from that place without dejection, it was probably because he was happy at least to have escaped and to have found the hidden path back to the dreadful doorway. Finally, since I am always eager to put your affairs in the best and most fortunate light, I hope that this trip of yours, necessary, brief, and your only one, will not harm you, but may prove to be of great profit. For what else, if I may mix the fabulous with the serious, does Homer's Achilles seek when, to be made invulnerable to steel, he is carried to the land of the dead and is bathed in the waters of the underworld — what else do you seek than that your solid virtue, tossed about in the great flood of vice, may harden in its hatred of its opposite,[6] may gather strength and become completely invulnerable to the barbs of human passion? I agree; I applaud; I approve; but don't go back. Seneca says: "we ought to choose a place not only healthy for one's body but also for one's character."[7]

---

[5] See above, p. 11.

[6] Petrarch held the medical notion that contraries are cured by contraries: "Vetus medicorum regula est, contraria contrariis curari." *Fam*. VII, 17, Rossi II, 134.

[7] *Ad Lucilium epistulae morales*, LI, 4; Petrarch also uses the line in the *De vita solitaria*, I, iii, 2 (Zeitlin tr., p. 127). Seneca's whole letter is about the immorality of Baiae, "a place to be avoided," he says, because of the noise, the raucous parties, and the drunks wandering on the beach.

That place against which I warn you is unwholesome for
both body and mind, and is completely unworthy of you.
Its way of life has nothing to commend it. Therefore, keep
an everlasting gulf between you and it; let others go to
the place who want to learn those arts of which an infinite
number of practitioners are there. You stay home. Hold
fast to your way of life and to that most distinguished
see which your virtue has brought you, though you deserve
a more distinguished one still. But if, since there is an
inclination in all of us to desire a decent change (and indeed
some erudite friends of mine are convinced that the pleasure
we get in being continually on the go is the one piece of
evidence we have of our celestial origin) — if you really
feel like traveling, then come to us: see Rome, Milan,
Venice, Florence, see your Padua, see Bologna where you
spent your youth in honourable studies and embellished
your native character with the Italic arts. Indeed, go as far as
the Indies if you like, only do not look upon Babylon; do
not descend to the living inferno.

15

This is a letter written in reply to someone in Avignon who
had much to complain about the place and who urged Petrarch
in Milan to stay away. He himself seems to be stuck in the
papal capital; he would like to leave, but cannot. There, is
virtually no evidence to assist in his identification.

It is impossible to say in a few words how closely your
advice coincides with my own feelings. It is certainly not
hard to choose between the best and the worst, so I
gladly shun what you urge me to avoid, and readily embrace

what you urge me to do — as they say, "I bow to your opinion,"[1] nor shall I abandon it unless by chance some great change in my affairs absolutely forces me to. I certainly fear no great change here; nor do I hope for any there, where if there seemed to be or had really been any who loved virtue, they either died long ago or abandoned the place, or else have now learned in that school of crime to hate the true and the good. "They are become corrupt and abominable in their works; there is none that does good, no, not even one" (Ps. 13, 1). I am referring to those upon whom Fortune had bestowed gifts all the more liberally so that they might be doers of good; but a deep-seated iniquity, hungering after crime, aroused by devilish suggestions, and in insolent disregard of the oracles of heaven, then led them in their perversity to prefer being evil and vicious.

But you who urge me so, what are your own plans? But then, what good is planning? Nowhere else is rational thought less fruitful. That's the once place on earth where there is no room for thoughtful counsel, where everything goes round aimlessly and without purpose. And among all the innumerable miseries of that place, there is this final trick: that everything is smeared with birdlime,[2] and is covered with hooks and nets, so that just when you think you have escaped you find yourself more tightly held and bound. There is no light anywhere, no one to lead you, no sign to guide you along the twisted paths, but only gloom on all sides and confusion everywhere. It is only too true, this is Babylon, that powerful chaos of things — "a vast night of

---

[1] *Pedibus in sententiam tuam eo.* The recipient must have known enough Roman law to recognize the expression.

[2] A sticky substance made from mistletoe, smeared on twigs and branches to capture birds.

crime," to quote Lucan.[3] A night of eternal darkness, I may
add, devoid of stars, in which dawn never comes, and where
deeds, moreover, are performed in deep and perpetual
shadows, with unceasing difficulties, infinite pain, undying
distaste, and with a furious upheaval of tempers as violent
as the gorge of the Rhone or the bluster of Circe and
Boreas. Think of them not as persons but as particles of
dust hurled by the wind. Confess that it is not so much
the city they inhabit that is evil, as they themselves who
are vile and deceitful. As a matter of fact, the features of
both people and place look the same: repulsive, offensive,
deformed. Upon each, as upon Pharaoh and Egypt, you can
understand an angry God "sending the fierceness of his
anger, his wrath and indignation and trouble, by sending
evil angels" (Ps. 77, 49). David's curse weighs upon no
people more than upon this one: "Let them be as chaff
before the wind, and let the angel of the Lord chase them;
let their way be dark and slippery, and let the angel of the
Lord persecute them" (Ps. 34, 5-6).

16

The person to whom Petrarch wrote this letter was a Roman,
and also a member of the Colonna family to judge from Petrarch's
reference to his relationship to Cardinal Giovanni Colonna. He
apparently had written to Petrarch in Milan to tell him of his
decision to leave Avignon, where presumably he was employed
in the papal court, and to return to his native Rome — news
which Petrarch received with much enthusiasm. These few clues
suggest that Petrarch's correspondent was probably Stefano

---

[3] *De bello civili,* VII, 571.

Colonna, a notary in the papal court, one of Petrarch's many friends in Avignon whom we know about from several other letters of his, and who seems to have shared Petrarch's aversion for the papal capital. It was to him, for instance, that Petrarch wrote the letter cited above in the Introduction: "No need to speak of where you live — they call it little Rome, I call it the newest Babylon; its reputation is well known not only to those nearby, but even to the Arabs and the Indians."

Oh, if you only knew how much your departure filled me with joy — or rather, your return, for to set out for one's homeland is to return. I could have had from you absolutely no news more welcome! Other decisions about the future belonged to Fortune, but it is to your own credit that with so much to hope for, under the weight of so many obligations, and despite so much contrary advice, you made up your mind on your own to flee that foulest sink of all crimes, and escape from those "grown fat from the pure blood, kicking against the Lord" (Deut., 32, 14-5), no "fishers of men" (Matt., 4, 19) but rather of pleasures and money. At the same time you were determined to revisit, being at long last better advised, that half-destroyed but still-to-be-feared citadel of the earth, that most holy head of the world, a head still glorious with its unkempt crown of white hair.[1] You have done the best thing I can think of, by wishing no longer to deny our mother-city the sight of such a son, and deciding that your unhappy prison was no longer worthy of your presence. "How I feared that the realms of Libya might have harmed you."[2] But with what joy do I now hear that you are freed from the foul and sorrowful confusion of that inescapable labyrinth, never (if you have any trust in me) to fall into

[1] Rome.
[2] *Aeneid*, VI, 694; also cited in *De vita solitaria*, I, v, 5 (Zeitlin tr., p. 167).

the same snare again while matters remain as they are. And
if repose, pleasure, freedom, life or glory are things you
hold dear, then you will be even more thankful for divine
grace and your good luck. "The Lord spoke once" (Job,
33,14), and he decreed at one stroke your fate and that
of all mortals who now live, who have ever lived, or who
will live in the future. Let all ambition cease! Say to God:
"my lot is in your hands" (Ps. 30, 16), and do not abandon
your course, once chosen, no matter how hard it is, no
matter how arduous and difficult. You will go unhindered
to the calm harbour without being held back by the slow
spite of evil men. They will languish in their own sins,
parched and thirsting like Tantalus[3] midst their evilly
acquired riches, and will marvel at your calm while you
happily enjoy divine gifts whatever your circumstances. They
will then realize that Fortune has no real hold over one of
steadfast and noble character. Just as they will spend their
brief, anxious and inglorious days in deep shadows, so both
their lives and their reputations will come to the same end.
Leave them to the vengeance of the Furies; leave them to
be rent by the terrible claws of their own crimes! By their
fate they will vindicate you, and all good men, and a world
despoiled and oppressed at their hands. If there is any true
prophecy anywhere, here it is: "that God, the Lord of
vengeance, may show himself" (Ps. 93, 1) and "bring abundant
retribution to those who act proudly" (Ps. 30, 24). "For
his is the vengeance, and he will repay them that their foot
will slide. The day of their calamity is at hand; their time
is hastening" (Deut., 32, 35).

---

[3] Tantalus was punished for his crimes by standing in water up to his chin
with fruit-laden trees over his head; when he got thirsty and tried to drink,
the water disappeared, and when he reached for the fruit the wind blew it away.

I am reminded of something I said many years ago to our late friend (the best, if I may say so, of a bad lot),[4] to whom you were related by blood, I by friendship and service: that the day of reckoning was not far off when, with the patience of God and men stretched to the limit, the proud way of life of that crowd would be overthrown and ended. I recall that when he (who, as you know, was gentle even in anger), with a rueful smile, hopefully attributed to me the blindness rather than the insight of Tiresius,[5] and threw at me the phrase from the Gospel: "Simon, I have prayed for you that your faith fail not" (Luke, 22, 32), I answered even more flippantly that I wasn't talking about a failure of faith, but about the downfall of those who had undermined faith, which would therefore be an increase of faith.

Now serious, he turned to me and said: "Hush; even if true, it's no fault of ours."

But look how many days have now gone by since then! As things now stand, I think he would call me a prophet if he were still alive. Now we have reached the end. The Roman race, the human race, has been humiliated enough. Virtue and truth have been despised long enough. Piety has been in exile and religion trampled upon long enough. And long enough — too long — has unworthy barbarism reigned. All things find their proper place, whether they like it or not; the end of this humiliation and overlong mockery is at hand. When I see it, my life will be complete.

[4] Petrarch is here referring to his old patron, Cardinal Giovanni Colonna.

[5] A legendary blind seer from Thebes.

17

The last three letters of the collection were all addressed to Francesco Nelli, but were never sent. Nelli had gone to Avignon on behalf of the newly elected abbot of San Salvi in Florence. On September 8, 1357, he wrote to Petrarch in Milan echoing the theme of Avignon as another labyrinth, "the world's cesspool." At the end of the letter he mentioned that he had found four good friends there which made life bearable. He wrote again on March 19, 1358, complaining that he had not yet received any reply. In fact, however, Petrarch had written a reply, letter 17, which, on rereading, he decided not to send for fear that it would fall into the wrong hands.

Letter 17 was probably written during the last months of 1357. Letter 18, implying that Nelli had been in Avignon longer than one might have expected, was probably not written until well on the next year. Like letter 17 it was not sent either. Probably it was never intended to be sent, but rather deliberately written for the collection. It provides a good example of Petrarch's narrative art, as well as an expression of the theme of the old lecher which pops up more than once in his work.

Letter 19, written in 1358 or 1359, begins on a note of elation that Nelli has finally left Avignon. Like the previous two letters, it too was not sent. But rather than leave the collection at that, Petrarch added an appendix to the letter addressed to the emperor Charles IV as a final plea to put Italian affairs in order by reestablishing the papacy in Rome.

No matter where you may go you remain the same, and you delight me as always. I am renewed by your sweet affection which never changes, your comforting words rich in their variety, whether they come "from the east or the west or the desert hills," since though "God is the judge, and he puts down one and raises up another" (Ps. 74, 7-8), nevertheless he preserves you as the comforting breeze of my cares, always modest, always lofty, always loving, breathing gently from whatever direction.

I hardly know what first to reply to your letter. It overflows with the truest and most serious comments. The fountain of your divine eloquence, springing from an arid and dusty land devoid of every good — a land, to use the words of the prophet king, "dry and thirsty, where no water is" (Ps. 62,3) — has filled my eyes, my ears and my spirit with a wonderful joy. Not even the barrenness of your new abode has been able to stop the ceaseless flow of your talent. I do not know whether to grieve that Fate should now have suddenly snatched you from that most flourishing[1] land where you were born and raised up from the cradle, and by a sudden turn of events carried you off from the country of your forefathers to a distant land and people, or to give thanks that she has not allowed your judgement to be overwhelmed by false notions or opinions and to be led away from the truth. For to one of such talent nothing about humanity should go unknown.[2] You could perhaps have gone off the track, you could have respected and put your trust in those to whom, as the saying goes, "nothing counts but money."[3] But now the facts before you will take the place of suppositions, and you will no longer put your trust in anything other than your own eyes, your own experience.

Look, now you can see with your own eyes, you can feel with your own hands, what this newest of Babylons is really like — burning, seething, repulsive, frightening. Neither that Babylon on the Nile which Cambyses built nor the older royal Babylon of Semiramis in Assyria matches it. Having

---

[1] *Florentissima*, i.e. Florence.
[2] A reminiscence of *Homo sum; humani nil me alienum puto* in TERENCE, *Heautontim.* I, i, 25. The expression was a medieval commonplace.
[3] OVID, *Fasti,* I, 217.

vanquished even the rivers of the lower world, the Cocytus
and the Acheron, the Rhone has certainly surpassed the Nile
and the Euphrates. Whatever faithlessness and fraud, whatever harshness and haughtiness, whatever shamelessness and
unbridled lust you have anywhere heard or read about,
whatever impiety and immorality is or was ever to be found
scattered about in the world, you may see it there all piled up,
all heaped up. As for greed and ambition, why bother saying
anything; it is clear that the first has established there the
throne of its kingdom, from where it strips and plunders the
entire world, while the second dwells nowhere else.

On all of this I considered a short time ago writing you
not a letter but a book,[4] to prevent a friend being deceived
by things well-known to me since my childhood. Long ago,
while I was strangely and unhappily stuck there, you were
there too. There, just as gold may be found in the muck —
or better, refined in the fire — I first found your friendship,
brighter than any gold. Even so, your lack of experience at
the time, your less developed judgement, and the shortness
or your stay disguised the reality. Besides, from what it was
then there has been an infinite change for the worse. Well,
you are now back there, riper in years, maturer in judgement,
and for a stay not only sufficient, or even excessive, but if I
am not mistaken drawn out to the point of disgust, so that
you who are quite familiar with all that is good will not stray
after all that is bad; you who have always loved virtue will
rouse your spirit by a hatred of vice to love virtue all the more
ardently, which is better still; and so that, if you devote yourself
completely to Christ as you have always done, the very sight
of the wickedness of his enemies will be a great spur to your
piety and faith.

[4] The work on the corruption of Avignon which he never wrote.

Look — you see a people not only opposed to Christ but, what is worse, rebelling against Christ while under his banner. They are servants of Satan, swollen with the blood of Christ, acting wantonly and saying: "our lips are our own; who is our Lord?" (Ps. 11, 5). A hard-hearted people, impious, haughty, famished, thirsting, with gaping beaks, sharp teeth, crooked claws, shifty feet, stone breasts, steel hearts, leaden wills, honeyed voices — a people to whom are properly applied, you would say, not only the words of the evangelist and the prophet: "This people honours me with their lips, but their heart is far from me" (Mark, 7, 6; Isaiah, 29, 3); but also the words of Judas Iscariot, who betrayed the Lord and kissed him and said: "Hail, master" (Matt., 26, 49); and of the Jews, who dressed him in purple, crowned him with thorns, struck him and spat upon him, bitterly jeered at him, and on bent knees mockingly honoured him and hailed him: "Hail, king of the Jews" (Mark, 15, 18; Matt., 27, 29). In a savage judgement they decreed that he was neither God nor king, and deserved neither divine nor human honours, but rather that he was "guilty of death" (Matt., 26, 66), a blasphemer who merited blows and execution. What else, I ask, goes on daily among these enemies of Christ, these Pharisees of our own time? Day and night they exalt Christ's name with the highest praises, they vest him in purple and gold, they deck him with gems, they salute him and prostrate themselves before him in worship, and meanwhile they buy him and sell him, hold an auction on him, crown him with thorns of base wealth as though with his eyes thus veiled he will not see, befoul him with spittle from the filthiest mouths, taunt him with their viperous hissing, and wound him with the lance of their poisonous deeds. With all their strength they drag him again and again to Calvary

— scoffed at, naked, helpless, scourged — and to blasphemous applause they nail him once again to the cross.

And — oh, the shame, the grief, the indignity of it all! — Rome, as it is said, is today in the hands of such people, while those who used to withstand them now suffer under their yoke. They claim her[5] for themselves with such contempt that they disdain to look upon what they wish to possess. At one time there was so much blood spilled in the world on her behalf, so many great leaders fallen, so many armies destroyed; but now I do not know how many disorderly and disreputable peasants rule her as they please, and tear at her without anyone trying to stop them, as though she were some enemy prize.

Oh foolish and wasteful prince![6] Had you no thought for the work that went into making that empire which you so casually threw away? Silly youths are used to squandering what they get from their fathers without thinking, of course, where or how their inheritance was put together — though, to be honest, the memory of the poverty and hardship it took never puts much of a check on wastefulness and pleasure-seeking. But you, you were a mature man. What were you doing? Where did you think you were? If all you wanted was to be thought generous you could have given away your private possessions, handed around your own inheritance, leaving intact for your successors that of the empire of which you were simply the custodian. I do not know whether or not it was in your power, but what in fact you did was to pass the administration of the state, founded so long ago by other hands, to the hands of those who were humble but are now haughty. It was about this that someone quipped,

---

[5] Rome.

[6] Now addressing the emperor Constantine the Great (d. 337), with reference to the famous Donation of Constantine.

rather cleverly: "Rome, your servants were lords of lords, now your lords are servants of servants." God, what I might say to you, given the chance! But I do not know whether or not you hear these words; for that matter it would make no difference if you do, for you made it impossible to change anything even if you were to return. To restore anything you have to be more of a builder than a wrecker.

You, oh Christ, you who can change things, you from whom all empires on earth, in heaven, or in hell are held at your will, you who, even in silence, hear this complaint which is not just my own but is made especially on behalf of all your people, hearken to us if it is just, we pray. I know indeed that it is written: "If I regard iniquity in my heart, the Lord will not hearken to me" (Ps. 65, 18). Oh Christ, you see the real truth of things; we have only a hesitant opinion. But of this at least we may be certain, that what we ask of you is reasonable. For we have many burdens on us, and a particularly crushing one is that we are bowed down under a rule which is not only hard and ignorant but is detestable and inimical. Thus in us is the psalm confirmed to the letter: "You have turned us back from the enemy, and those who hate us plunder us for themselves; you have given us like sheep to be eaten" (Ps. 43, 11-12). The words that then follow are known. This alone is enough for us to complain and lament over. For if you look at it, what have we who used to be lords of nations been turned into, if not sheep to be eaten? If only we were merely sheep to be sheared, or milked — but no, we are sheep to be eaten. We let ourselves be chewed, consumed, devoured by those who, if we began to resist, would themselves seem like sheep before lions. They would not seem to be as outstanding as they have for so long. At present our lethargy is greater than

their audacious cowardice; quite wickedly they feed upon
our tolerance while at the same time hating it. And what
will amaze you even more, we whom they despise on the
surface they fear deep down. They pretend contempt, but it
is really fright. There are a thousand proofs of their hatred,
a thousand of their fear. Here is an example to demonstrate
both at once. Though it used to be secret, nevertheless it
came out in the open and was known not only in Babylon
but far and wide.

It was back in the days when that Pontifex Maximus[7] had
decided to destroy the province of Italy and especially this
city of Milan with a senile expedition of priestly troops.
Thus did the father of Christians rage with unrelieved hatred
against a Christian land and a Christian city as though it
were not Italy, but Syria or Egypt — not Milan, but
Damascus or Memphis. For this sacred and pious undertaking he appointed one of the members of the sacred
college of fathers, whom many said was his son — and
a marked resemblance, as well as his foul temper, added
strength to the rumour.[8] The pope sent him into this land
in no apostolic fashion but like a brigand, equipped not
with the signs of virtues and miracles, but with the ensigns

---

[7] Pope John XXII (1316-1334).

[8] Cardinal Bertrand du Poujet, papal legate in northern Italy from 1320 to 1334,
whose campaign against Milan during this time Petrarch refers to. Just a few
years before writing this letter, however, when Bertrand died in 1352, Petrarch
had this to say of him in a letter to Philippe de Cabassoles: "While I was
writing these words, the cardinal bishop of Ostia [Bertrand] has been dying;
by the time you read them, he will have breathed his last. Death comes to him
at a ripe age, but too soon, it seems to me, for the public welfare." It has
been demonstrated that Bertrand was neither the son, as Petrarch says here,
nor even the nephew, as Giovanni Villani says, of pope John. See the article
by G. MOLLAT in *Dictionnaire d'histoire et de géographie ecclésiastiques*, VII (Paris,
1935), 1068-1069.

of the military camp and remarkable legions — like another Hannibal, not another Peter. In the war, omnipotent God in his own way "resisted the proud and favoured the humble" (James, 4, 6) and openly fought on the side of justice.

Now, there was one member of that same flock who had an insatiable hatred for us, a man of unlimited pride whose face I knew when I was a boy and whose character I despised as much as a child could. One day this man, who was closer to the pope than all the others, entered the anteroom and found the pope worried and anxious about the news. The attack launched in the hope of taking this city was bogged down at its edge. The city had no walls, but it was defended by outstanding soldiers and splendid leaders, the best kind of walls. Often the defenders broke up the lines of their besiegers, and soon their prisons overflowed with crowds of captives while the fields grew rich with the bodies of the slain.[9]

This was the state of affairs, then, when he saw the pope more downcast than usual. Taking advantage of the close familiarity he enjoyed, he began: "I wonder, holy father, why it is that you who are so astute in everything else don't know what to do about this one thing which is of the greatest importance to us."

At these words, the pope raised his head, which had been bowed in grave concern.

"Go on," he said, "what is it?"

That oustanding adviser then continued: "I realize that you seek nothing more than the devastation of Italy. To this we devote our energy, our wealth, our every thought; for this we pour out almost all the church's treasure, and are now

[9] The siege of Milan began on June 11, 1323, and ended on July 28.

caught in a trap unless we try some other road. Look at
that huge engine of war, the spearhead of our forces; it is
now blunted by the very gates of Milan. What flatterers had
assured you was very like any one of our own cities has turned
out to be superior to them all. When shall we ever conquer
Italy? We've been beaten by a single city! But if you wish,
there is a far easier way open to you."

"What way?" asked the pontiff. "Speak, and be quick
about it. For this is my goal, this is my desire, this is the one
thing for which I'd sell my body and soul."

"Everything is in your power," the cardinal replied. "Whatever you order is done. So why not remove both papacy
and empire from the city of Rome and Italy, and transfer
the papacy to our homeland in Cahors, the empire to Germany?
It takes no effort. Just give the word and it's done. There's
no need for armies, in which we are badly deficient.
You'll conquer your enemies with a word. Say it. You'll
decorate us with new honours by transferring the highest
office to us, and you'll deprive that hated nation of its twin
splendour."

At these words the pope rose, a bitter laugh welling up
from his anger.

"You misled me," he said. "I hadn't realized before that
you were crazy. Aren't you aware, you ignorant fool, that by
going down this road you thought you had so neatly paved,
I and my successors would become mere bishops of Cahors
and the emperor, whoever he might be, a German prefect,
while whoever remained in Rome to rule in spiritual matters
would be pope or if in temporal matters emperor? Thus while
you think you're wiping out the name of Italy you raise it up
and restore it to its old dignity. Let's hang on to the reins
of the papacy while heaven allows, and do our best to stop

the Italians' taking back at some time what is their right. How long we can prevent it I don't know. But let's not argue about titles; whether we like it or not, Rome will remain the head."

At this that clever fool blushed. As for me, though I deplore the pope's purpose I am compelled to commend his insight. Though he burned with unmerited hatred of us, nevertheless he remembered and recognized where that eminence had been founded from the height of which they have displayed their presumption; he saw that to damage the foundations would bring disaster. And so he thought it wise to keep quiet and to enjoy his spoils in silence like a thief. I do not know whether this story has been written up by anyone else;[10] I have given it in this much detail in order that, if it is already known to you, you will see that I know it too; but if not known to you, you may learn it from me, so that you who know of the ancient past may not be ignorant of the present.

Now these people rule us. They plunder us, hate us, pretend to despise us but really fear us. Even if any one of us, like a clean stream mixing into a muddy torrent, has been enrolled among that number, taken in out of fear or shame rather than from any considered judgement, he has long since lost his native hue, and has been completely dissolved into the nature and foreign ways of the many others.[11] There is nothing at all left now but to pray to Christ that if our punishment is not yet sufficient he might at least consider his see,[12] take it from these people, and hand it to others of whom the human

---

[10] It wasn't.

[11] If any Italian is taken into the college of cardinals, he soon becomes just as bad as the others.

[12] The papacy.

race need not repent and be ashamed. For they are just as bad as I say they are — no, that's not right; I cannot say how bad they are. Thus the state began to sink from where it once was down to the very depths of indignity and infamy, starting from the time when the holy and powerful church, once Roman, now Avignonese, began to touch the stars with its crown and revolve the heavens with a finger — a church to which Judas will be admitted if he brings with him his thirty pieces of blood money, while Christ the pauper will be turned away from the gate. There is no Christian who does not know that this is so, who does not grieve, or who would excuse it. But while one person waits for the other, you can see how the evils increasingly go unpunished. What at the outset had been a wound capable of treatment has finally grown putrid; for, I confess, the ugly sore had begun to fester even before our own time, as we know from our forefathers. Often, however, an incompetent doctor, and often too the headstrong patient itself, contributed to the unchecked growth of an infection which had been more annoying, you might say, than fatal. Now it's coming to a head, and all the puss is bursting forth in our day. What a mournful thing, if there were not one kind of comfort midst such great evils.

Let me tell you now, therefore, what I said some time ago to one who alone of all those who belong to that evil flock was deserving of a better pasture. And he agreed with me completely, though what I said applied to him too — because of his status and origin,[13] mind, not because of his morals. Given, I said, that the governments of mortals are themselves mortal, if the passage of time demands that the two luminaries[14]

[13] In other words, he was a cardinal in status and French in origin.
[14] The papacy and the empire.

of the world be extinguished and the two swords blunted, though we hoped that each, and certainly one, would be preserved according to divine promises (and we need not despair that after they have been utterly destroyed all these things will rise again all the higher) — if, as I said, we in our day have to face the serious threat that these high authorities will be destroyed, God! how glad I am that whilst the light and strength of these powers will have remained in our hands so great a change came under aliens, and that so great a blame is to be shared by the barbarian Germans, savage and fierce, and the barbarian French, soft and effeminate.

After listening to this without being at all offended by my liberty, he replied, "You have spoken with much weight and frankness — possibly too violently for other ears, but as far as I am concerned most courageously and truthfully, as befits you. So that you won't think that perhaps I am ignorant of the truth or hold some different opinion, I do not doubt, nor do I think that anyone can doubt, that our two Clements[15] have weakened the church more in a few years than your seven Gregories[16] could make up for in several centuries." Having spoken, he heaved a sigh.

Christ Jesus, we have been carried away enough "by the zeal of your house" (Ps. 68, 10; John, 2, 17); no fouler digression under the sun could have led my pen astray. I must return to my subject.

Well then, my friend, either because Fate envied you your quiet or thought that you needed instruction, you came to

---

[15] Clement V (1305-1314) and Clement VI (1342-1352).

[16] There had been ten popes named Gregory, eight of whom were Italians. But since one of these, Gregory VIII, died just two short months after election, this may account for Petrarch's count of seven.

this people as a foreign traveller, not to say an exile, on business rather than for pleasure. As a result you deprived yourself of your plan of reading and me mine of writing.[17] Surely you have nothing now to learn from me or anyone else about Babylon on the Rhone, or what it is like to be exiles of Sion by the rivers of Babylon. Your recent letter about the place struck me as being all the more splendid for your seeming to have examined the secret things of that sewer from top to bottom, and to have thoroughly inspected all the hidden corners of its labyrinth. You learned the truth with much disgust, I imagine, and with much torment. You had the consolation — a matter of some pleasure for you, some envy for me — that midst that great gloom of vice, so you write, you "enjoyed the friendship of those four wonderful men, like just so many brilliant stars."[18] I do not know what holds them there — whether some crime of their forefathers (for they themselves, I know, are the best and purest of men), some great disappointment of life's hope, some blow of Fortune, some sad necessity, as if — but let me explain what I mean at least in poetic terms — as if, I say, they were sunbeams in a sewer, exposing in their rays every obscenity of the place while yet remaining unsoiled by the surrounding filth.

18

Why do you dally there? Or is it more than dalliance, and you are in fact being held, forced to remain against your will? I hope

[17] Yet another reference to the work he intended to devote to Avignon. Why write about it, he says, since you can now see it for yourself.
[18] Guido Sette, with whom Petrarch grew up and went to school; Laelius, an old friend whom Petrarch first met in the household of Giacomo Colonna; Stefano Colonna; and Socrates to whom he dedicated the *Familiares*.

so. I prefer to think of you as under some compulsion rather than giving way to weakness. It is not your nature to be apathetic; you have a lively talent, a fiery mind, a marvellous energy. But what are these, if the obstacle be stronger than their force? For great strength is as nothing when confronted by greater strength, and all things give way to Necessity. She drew you to Babylon; it is she who holds you there. It is hard, but it must be borne. It is the nature of the place. Every blessing is lost there, freedom before all else; then in quick succession repose, joy, hope, faith, charity, the soul — huge losses, these, but in the Kingdom of Avarice no harm is done provided one's money is safe. There the hope for a future life is called a kind of empty fable, the accounts of hell are considered so much make-believe, and the resurrection of the body, the end of the world, and Christ's coming again to sit in judgement are called old wives' tales.[1] Truth is madness, abstinence the mark of a rustic, modesty an enormous disgrace, while sinful licence is called greatness of soul, the best of freedoms. The more corrupt one's life, the more illustrious it is; the more a man sins, the greater his glory. A good name is valued more cheaply than dirt. The highest reputation is a reputation for wealth. Here you have, to the extent possible in a few words, a description of the nature of that sacred city. But what you read in this letter today is no more than what you may read on the faces of those people every day. No pen, no talent, is equal to depicting their life.

But the first thing of all to be lost there, as I said, is freedom. Whoever crosses that threshhold immediately ceases to be his own man. From that moment on he is neither left in

[1] Here as elsewhere Petrarch bears witness to the spread of religious scepticism to Avignon during the fourteenth century.

peace nor allowed to withdraw, but is whirled about, worn out and swallowed up in fruitless effort. Divine mercy rescues a few from the place on the grounds that they love Jerusalem and have come to hate Babylon. This remains my hope for you. Otherwise, I believe it is all up with you; I can see you held fast by the deep, clutching bog (Ps. 68, 3). Meanwhile I blame Necessity and Fortune, rather than your desire or your considered decision, for your remaining there this long. And your stay, which I hate so much, I willingly excuse. For if you were possibly at fault for going there, surely now your staying there is no fault, but rather the punishment and expiation of the fault. Well now, since many have often learned a great deal while in prison, what is there to stop you while in your bondage from learning something from which you may forever profit? Some things are best learned by considering their opposites. For instance, if a mathematics teacher finds that his pupil seems incapable of seeing some point, he often puts forward a false proposition by rejecting which the pupil may find his way to the truth. Now in your case you have always been accustomed to care deeply about religion and honour, the first of which raises the hopeful soul to the sight of him of whom the Psalmist says: "Seek his face evermore" (Ps. 104, 4), while the face of the other "is such that if you were to cast your eyes upon it, it would inflame the mind with marvellous love, as Plato says,"[2] although what the soul sees ought not to be loved the less. If now you lack anything to complete your knowledge of either religion or honour, bend your every effort, alert your ears, direct your eyes, turn your attention to their very opposites. Do you want to know the beauty of God? Then look how great is the obscenity of his enemies. You need not seek them far; they dwell in Babylon where

---

[2] CICERO, *De offic.*, I, 15.

every street crawls with the worms. Do you want to see the comeliness and splendour of honour? Then look how great is the filth of wickedness; there are examples of every kind before your eyes. Wherever you look you will see those things by hating which you may be able to grow firmer in your love both of God and of virtue.

Now Babylon, foulest of cities, rejoice at least for being the opposite of the mistress of virtues. Rejoice, I say, and take pride that you have been found useful for something — you, the enemy of the good, the dwelling-place and refuge of evil, seated on the savage banks of the Rhone, famous — or rather infamous — whore "with whom the kings of the earth have committed fornication" (Apoc. 17, 1-2; 18, 3). You indeed are the very one whom the holy evangelist saw in his vision. It is you, I say, and no other, who "sits upon many waters" (Apoc. 17, 1), either to be interpreted literally as girdled by three rivers,[3] or as a heap of temporal goods and riches on which you sit, lascivious and heedless, unmindful of the riches of heaven, or, as he who saw it said, "the waters on which the whore sits are peoples and nations and tongues" (Apoc. 17, 15). Look again at the description: "the woman was arrayed in purple and scarlet colour and decked with gold and precious stones and pearls, having a gold cup in her hand full of abominations and filthiness of her fornication" (Apoc. 17, 4). Do you recognize yourself, Babylon? If he was right in saying that there was written on her forehead "Babylon the Great" (Apoc. 17, 5), then you are Babylon the Small. Small indeed in the circumference of your walls, but in vice and the corruption of souls, in infinite greed and the heaping up of every wickedness, you are not just great, but rather huge, immense. And

---

[3] Rhone, Durance and Sorgues rivers.

certainly the words that follow apply to you alone and to no other: "Babylon, the mother of harlots and abominations of the earth" (Apoc. 17, 5). You are the impious mother of the foulest offspring, seeing that every abomination anywhere on earth, every harlot, is born of you, and that you continually give birth to them, your womb being always swollen, full and heavy with them. If you now still pretend otherwise, then hear the rest: "And I saw the woman drunken with the blood of the saints, and with the blood of the martyrs of Jesus" (Apoc. 17, 6). Why are you silent?

Either show that it is another who is drunken with this blood, or at least deny completely, if you can, that you are she. For we cannot doubt the truth of the vision of the evangelist and apostle. If when he saw you in the spirit he "wondered with great admiration" (Apoc. 17, 6), with how much wonder are we overcome, we who see you in the flesh? Indeed, from all "your fornications of which all the nations and the kings of the earth have drunk" (Apoc. 18, 3), and from all your abominations, what can you look forward to other than what John says: "Babylon the Great is fallen, is fallen, and is become the habitation of devils" (Apoc. 18, 2). The words that come next are well known. Truly, that is what you have become. For is a man who is damned, a man of desperate wickedness, any better than a devil? Truly you have become the habitation — the kingdom, rather — of devils who, though in human form, reign in you with their devilish arts.

But now you, my friend,[4] listen with the apostle to "another voice from heaven saying, come out of her, my people, that you be not partakers of her sins, and that you receive not of her

---

[4] Now addressing Nelli.

plagues. For her sins have reached unto heaven, and God has remembered her iniquities. How much she has glorified herself and lived deliciously, so much torment and sorrow give her: for she says in her heart, I sit a queen and am no widow and shall see no sorrow. Therefore shall her plagues come in one day, death, and mourning, and famine; and she shall be utterly burned with fire; for strong is the Lord God who judges her" (Apoc. 18, 4-8).

Listen to all these things which that apostolic text contains; listen and flee, if there is any way left open to you, and so keep your innocence from being overwhelmed in the downfall of the wicked and by the iniquities of Babylon, of which there is no measure, no number, no dimension, no estimate. I say nothing of Simon's heritage,[5] and that recent species of heresy of those who traffic in the gifts of the Holy Spirit. I say nothing of the mother of that evil, Avarice, which the apostle called Idolatry (Col. 3, 5). I say nothing of the practitioners of each of these pestilences, the agents of the papal chamber, bustling about. I say nothing of the mindless cruelty of humanity, the arrogance which is forgetful of itself, nor of those human skins puffed up with empty vanity. Finally, I say nothing of those prodigies which a numb and truly destitute world can suffer only so long, like Enceladus buried under Mount Etna or Typheus under the island of Ischia.[6] About all of this it is too sorrowful and too gloomy to write. I hasten to things as laughable as they are hateful.

For who, I ask, would not be angered and at the same time amused at those grey-headed old sports, clad in togas which flow as broadly as their spirits frolic, so that nothing

[5] Simony, from Simon Magus.
[6] *Aeneid*, III, 578 ff.

seems further from the truth than that line from Vergil: "Old
age is frigid in love."[7] How hot are the old in love — how they
rush to it! Such forgetfulness of age, rank and strength! How
they burn with passion, how they hurry to every dishonour, as
though their every glory is not in Christ's cross but in
banquets and drinking bouts and what comes next on their
scandalous couches. How they cling to the hand of their
fleeting youth; they think that the one last reward of old age
is to do those things the young dare not do. Wild Bacchus and
the violence of the eastern Bacchae have endowed them with
such energetic spirits.[8] Oh you Ligurian and Campanian vines,
oh you sweet young shoots, oh you dark Indian shrubs,
created for the honest pleasure and delight of men, to what
uses have you been put! To what great downfall and destruction
of men's souls have you been directed! Satan looks upon
all this and rejoices, shares in their dance with delight, sits
among the old men and the young girls, looks upon them
and is amazed that they do even more than he prompts
them to do. And to keep any tiredness from stealing over them,
he goads the ageing limbs and blows up love's dying fire with
the exotic bellows[9] which everywhere fans the flame of filthy
passion. I omit the debauchery, the ravishment, the incest,
the adultery which are now the pasttimes of priestly lewdness.
I say nothing of the husbands of the violated — they dare not
complain — forced not only to give up their ancestral
homes but to leave their homelands, and what is most
deplorable, compelled to take back their ravished wives
bearing the seed of others only to return them, after they

---

[7] *Georg.*, III, 97, where the reference, however, is to a horse.
[8] Too much drinking.
[9] Presumably the artificial stimulant of wine.

have been delivered, to satisfy their abusers yet again. All of this not only I know, but everyone does even if nothing is said — though the fact speaks for itself, for indignation is now greater than fear, and grief has overcome the threats of the lustful. All these things, I say, I pass over. Indeed, today I would rather provoke you to laughter than to wrath. For anger which cannot be satisfied turns in on itself and destroys its own harbourer.

Well now, there was a certain little old fellow of that crowd who deserves a place in all the annals. The man was as lusty as a goat. If there is anything lustier and smellier than a goat, he was it. He dared not sleep alone, fearing either mice or ghosts.[10] He found nothing more depressing or more wretched than celibacy. Daily he celebrated new nuptials, and was betrothed again and again in casual encounters, though he was as empty of mouth as he was full of years — he was well over seventy, with scarcely seven teeth left. He employed a hunter of young maidens who was one in a million, in every way equal to the demands of his master's lust. His traps and snares were to be found in all the streets and in all the houses, especially of the poor: here some money, there a necklace, here a few rings, there a little flattery, here the left-overs of some banquet, there all sorts of food — whatever deviousness captures the female fancy. Then he kept his fingers crossed, and meanwhile sang: for he was

[10] *Mures metuens seu lemures.* The play on words is lost in translation. It is a well-worn device, not often indulged in by Petrarch, but here used along with a number of others, e.g., the pointed ambiguity (he celebrated new nuptials), the diminutives *seniculus, misella, virguncula,* the exaggerated contrast (over seventy with scarcely seven teeth), the association with the animal world (lusty as a goat, an old wolf), all to announce, in effect, "look, I'm telling a funny story." See Ezio RAYMUNDI, "Una pagina satirica delle *Sine nomine,*" *Studi petrarcheschi,* VI (1956), 55-61.

in fact a cantor, though he had transferred his voice from the altar to the theatres and the bawdy houses. I knew the man, pointed out to me by the finger of the crowd. He was said to have been accustomed with his skills to entice a lot of game into the jaws of that old wolf.

This place holds a thousand funny stories. Here is one.

With many promises the fellow had worked on a wretched little maid — rather, little courtesan — in order to induce her to do the pleasure of his lord who was of high rank indeed and of great wealth but attractive neither in appearance nor because of his age. Need I say more? She agrees. And just like that Psyche of Lucius Apuleius, to be honoured in happy marriage,[11] she enters the chamber of a man unknown to her. As soon as he finds out about it the old man, impatient with delay, comes flying, and grabbing her by the elbows he fervently kisses her with trembling lips, nibbles her with his untoothed gums, and pants all the while to consummate the new union. Suddenly startled by the evil and smelly old creature, and terrified by his lurid looks, she cries out that she has come for a great and important prelate, not for an ugly and decrepit priest; no one is going to fool her; if anyone tries to use force on her she'll defend herself, with her hands as long as she can, then with her cries and screams; she isn't going to let herself be taken by such a dirty old man, not while there is a single breath left in her body! Screaming all the while, she wept copiously.

Closing up the tender mouth with his scabrous hand and his bristly, frothing face, he tries to keep her from crying and carrying on, and with confused mutterings and bumbling blandishments (for besides everything else he stuttered so

[11] *Met.*, V, 2-4.

much that no one could understand him) he tries to soothe
the unhappy girl. But when nothing will do, that truly
remarkable old fellow rushes out to the anteroom, snatches up
the red hat that marks off the conscript fathers from
everyone else, and clapping this mark of distinction on his
shiny bald head he cries, "Have no fear, my daughter, I'm
a cardinal, I'm a cardinal!" He then consoled the little lover
girl, hitherto weeping, with a down-payment and a promise
of more to come, and led her off to the marriage bed, under the
auspices not of Juno but of Tisiphone and Megaera.[12] That was
how Cupid's old veteran, that priest of Bacchus and Venus,
triumphed in his loves, not armed, but toga'ed and hatted.
Applaud. The fable is done.

It's a pity that you didn't know his man. He sang so
beautifully.

There are a thousand stories of him and the others, some
of which are not funny but are shameful, while some are
frightful and horrid.

Now go ahead, marvel that with leaders like this Christ is
well disposed to his people or that the state prospers.

---

[12] Juno was the goddess of marriage and the family. But Petrarch is telling of
no common marriage, so its goddesses are the Furies. There were three of
these, Tisiphone, Megaera and Alecto, to whom were ascribed the task of
punishing the dead (VERGIL, *Aeneid*, VI, 570-572; LUCAN, *De bello civili*, I, 572-577;
VI, 730). They are not often associated with marriage, but for one example
see CLAUDIAN, *In Rufinam*, I, 83-84:

> hac auspica taedae
> Oedipoden matri, natae iunxere Thyesten.

Under the auspices of Megaera, Oedipus married his own mother, Thyestes
his own daughter. Then, too, there is the misogynist Juvenal (whose pessimism
finds more than one echo in these pages of Petrarch): "Are you getting
married, Postumus? Tell me, what Tisiphone has driven you mad?" (*Sat.* VI,
28-29).

19

You have escaped; you have broken out; you have swum
to safety; you have flown free. Well done! I admit that I
feared for you; I feared that after your descent to the land of
the dead your soul would not rise again when it wanted to. I
knew that the "descent to Avernus was easy,"[1] the gate of the
labyrinth was wide, and that the way out was hard and
difficult to find. I said to myself: Oh, if my Alcides, oh if
my Theseus[2] might only return from the land of the dead!
Oh, that the weight of evils may not crush him, that the steel
chains of wickedness may not bind and shackle his feet, so
swift to pursue virtue. While I prayed, while I feared, you
emerged — thanks be to God who guides out of the
inferno the souls of them that trust in him. I hoped for you.
I called for you. I waited for you. Now you come. As soon,
therefore, as you return to this soil which had lent you to
the lower world, you will consecrate your propellant wings
to Christ — not to Phoebus, as Daedalus did — and take heed
never again to look upon Knossos. You should not tempt
Fortune too often. To run such a risk is dangerous. Though you
have escaped it this time, take care not to fall in again and not
come up. I hope you are never touched by the evil desire
to revisit those princes of darkness. Let all the gods and
goddesses, even the God of gods, abandon them, both the
living and the dead, to their evil, with their riches and
shameless deeds. Grown fat from the blood of the lamb of
heaven, they kick and rebel (Deut. 32, 15).

[1] *Aeneid,* VI, 126ff.
[2] A reference to Hercules and Theseus in the underworld. There is a brief
reminiscense in *Aeneid,* VI, 392.

Now that friend of mine[3] asks me to go there — much to my surprise, for he could not talk me into it even while you were still there. He acts in good faith, of course, but with little forethought, urging that I choose to live in Babylon, and to die there. Why should I? What is the point? So that I can see the good laid low, evil raised on high, eagles crawl, asses fly, foxes ride in triumph, crows in the citadels, doves in the dungpits, wolves running free, lambs in chains, Christ in exile, Antichrist enthroned, Beelzebub in the seats of justice? These are the sights to which I am summoned again. I shall not listen. They do not suit me; I do not suit them.

What a cruel and impious band of men, loving only themselves and doing that most wrongly and wickedly! Who will raise up this oppressed world once more? Who will avenge the distress of Rome? Who will reestablish the old ways, gather the scattered sheep, reprove the errant shepherds and lead them or drag them back to their proper place? Will there never be a limit to licence and crime? Or is it in vain that the Holy Spirit spoke thus through the prophet: "These things you have done and I kept silence. You mistakenly thought that I was like you; I shall reprove you and shall decide these things before your eyes. Consider this, you who are forgetful of God, lest I tear you to pieces and there be no one to deliver you" (Ps. 49, 21-22). Consider this, I say, consider this, you enemies of God. He speaks to you!

He speaks to the deaf and the sleeping. They will never hear if they are not awakened by the dreadful thunder or, if that is not enough, by the three-pronged lightning.

Let me now address you, greatest of the kings of our day.[4]

---

[3] Socrates.
[4] Though the letter is ostensibly addressed to Nelli, Petrarch turns here to address the emperor Charles IV.

I do not call you by name, since to name you goes against the title
of this book, and anyway the very magnitude of your affairs
and the greatness of your glory amply identify you. What need
is there for words when the matter speaks for itself? It is
right to believe that you have deserved the great victories
with which you have been blessed — you who, aside from the
justice of a case which pertains to you as prince, at all
events have strength enough to evict those slothful foxes
from dens which they have befouled and which do not belong
to them, and to rescue the bride of Christ from her filthy
bonds. And it is lawful for you to do so, I trust. You will
have the wishes of all the faithful for your perpetual good
fortune and for the desired outcome of what you undertake.
You alone will restore that shepherd,[5] bowed with age and
drowsiness and strong wine, to the old sanctuary, dragging
him by force, rebuking him with words, chastising him with
scourges, for he will never willingly leave his favourite haunts
and beloved brothels.[6] If by chance heaven does not give
you this role (though there is no one endowed with more
gifts, and no one more deserving of this one) others will
come, and the fouler their hand the sweeter the revenge. Many
such are on the increase everywhere: at long last Christ
may succour his anguished bride by the just attack of mercenaries,[7] by a healing plague,[8] by the merciful inclemency of the
heavens, finally by some manifest catastrophe, since the proud

---

[5] Pope Innocent VI (1352-1362).

[6] *Fornices amate,* another play on words, referring to the papal palace.

[7] Many of the mercenaries employed in the Hundred Years War were released
after the defeat of the French at Poitiers and the subsequent truce of 1356.
A large band overran papal territories in Provence in 1357, and pope Innocent VI
was forced to strengthen the walls of the city and hire soldiers to defend it.

[8] A reminiscence of the Black Death of 1348.

and hardened heart of Pharaoh remains untouched by threats and warnings.

Oh what have I said, what have I written, what have I been thinking of? Where has my tongue led me? How far has my pen gone? Perhaps I might say, like Job: "One thing have I said, would that I had not" (Job, 39, 55). However, I said it and now I cannot unsay it. Even if it be still possible to erase it, I have no wish to do so. So great is my love of truth, so great my hatred of evil, that I meanwhile forget every danger. In one thing, however, I shall follow the advice of that old prophet, for while there is still an infinite number of things that cry out to be said, and though I have run through only a very few of them, I shall now stop and, again like Job, "I shall put my hand over my mouth and add nothing more to these things" (Job, 39, 34-5). Amen.

BIBLIOGRAPHICAL NOTE

For the text of the letters I have used Paul Piur, *Petrarcas 'Buch ohne Namen' und die päpstliche Kurie* (Halle/Saale: Max Niemeyer, 1925). I am also heavily indebted to his extensive discussions of the addressees and dates of the letters.

I have consulted translations of the *Sine nomine*, in whole or in part, in the following works:

Victor Develay, *Pétrarque: Lettres sans titre* (Paris: Librairie des Biblio-
philes, 1885).

Orazio d'Uva, *Le Anepigrafe di Fr. Petrarca* (Sassari, 1895).

J.H. Robinson and H.W. Rolfe, *Petrarch, First Modern Scholar* (New York,
1898).

M.E. Cosenza, *Francesco Petrarca and the Revolution of Cola di Rienzo*
(Chicago: University of Chicago Press, 1913).

E.H. Wilkins, *Petrarch at Vaucluse* (Chicago: University of Chicago Press,
1958).

John E. Wrigley, "A Papal Secret known to Petrarch," *Speculum,* XXXIX
(1964), 613-634.

John E. Wrigley, "A Rehabilitation of Clement VI," *Archivum historiae
pontificiae,* III (1965), 127-138.

A complete manual of the correspondence of Petrarch is that of E.H. Wilkins, *Petrarch's Correspondence* (Medioevo e umanesimo, III), (Padua: Editrice Antenore, 1960).

Petrarch's *Familiares*, which I have frequently cited, are best consulted in the edition of V. Rossi, *Epistolae familiares,* 4 vols. (vol. 4 edited by U. Bosco) (Florence, 1926-1942).

INDEX